Woman-Killing in Juárez

Woman-Killing in Juárez

Theodicy at the Border

Rafael Luévano

ORBIS BOOKS

Maryknoll, New York 10545

Founded in 1970, Orbis Books endeavors to publish works that enlighten the mind, nourish the spirit, and challenge the conscience. The publishing arm of the Maryknoll Fathers and Brothers, Orbis seeks to explore the global dimensions of the Christian faith and mission, to invite dialogue with diverse cultures and religious traditions, and to serve the cause of reconciliation and peace. The books published reflect the views of their authors and do not represent the official position of the Maryknoll Society. To learn more about Maryknoll and Orbis Books, please visit our website at www.maryknollsociety.org.

Published by Orbis Books, Maryknoll, New York 10545–0302.

Manufactured in the United States of America.

Manuscript editing and typesetting by Joan Weber Laflamme.

Queries regarding rights and permissions should be addressed to: Orbis Books, P.O. Box 302, Maryknoll, New York 10545–0302.

Library of Congress Cataloging-in-Publication Data

Luévano, Rafael.
　Woman-killing in Juárez : theodicy at the border / Rafael Luévano.
　　　p. cm.
　Includes bibliographical references (p.).
　ISBN 978–1–57075–968–0 (pbk.)
　1. Suffering—Religious aspects—Christianity. 2. Violence—Religious aspects—Christianity. 3. Theodicy. 4. Women—Crimes against—Mexico—Ciudad Juárez. I. Title.
　BV4909.L84 2011
　231'.8—dc23

2011042230

*Este libro se lo dedico a la memoria
a todas las mujeres desaparecidas
y asesinadas en el norte de México.*

*Being attentive to God means hearing the
silence of those who have disappeared.*

—JOHANN BAPTIST METZ

Contents

PART II
THE CALL

Acknowledgments

I offer my admiration and thanks to the many surviving family members of the missing and murdered women in Juárez (and beyond). These persons often took great personal risk to share their firsthand experiences.

Many others offered support and assistance, and without their help this book would not be possible. Bishop Tod D. Brown must be acknowledged as more than generous and patient with me. *Gracias.* Many persons assisted me with field research in Juárez: Diana Washington, Arturo Bañuelas, Robert Almonte, Park Kerr, Jerry Horan, Katie Hubab, and Marvin Lucus. Additional thanks along these lines to José Luis Sierra, who also read and made corrections to the text. Richard Rodriguez offered me invaluable inspiration, direction, and support in the production of the work.

I offer loving thanks to my siblings, Linda, Michael, Mark, and Susan the librarian, who assisted with my research. Max Luévano-Molina helped out with his technical skills. Martin Escalante and Al Molina also deserve acknowledgment.

I am grateful for all the dear friends who gave me constant support: Austin Doran, Mary Rourke, Michael Bernstein, Frank Quevedo, Inez Quevedo, Leia Smith, Shelly Donelle, Ed Butorac, David Lavenau, Michael Kret, Victoria Carty, Joe Levin, Gary Levin, Fernando and Olga Niebla, Octavio Navaro, Roselio Lopez, Elva Rubalcaba, Hamid Shirvani, Mary Shulty, Juan Lara, Joyce and Mike Greenspan, Gary and Joe Levin, Dean and Ellie Snow, and Sharon Dixon.

I gratefully acknowledge my colleagues at Chapman University: Carmichael Peters, Jeanne Gunner, Roberta Lessor, Patrick Quinn, Luis Ortiz-Franco, Julye Bidmead, Marilyn J. Harran,

Marvin W. Meyer, Nancy Martin, Charles Hughes, Richard Ruppel, and Ron Farmer. I must also remember my theological colleagues and friends at various universities: Virgilio Elizondo, John Borelli, Barbara Reid, Nancy Piñeda-Madrid, Michael Joncas, Bill McDonough, and Jim Fredricks.

I thank my publisher, Robert Ellsberg. Susan Perry, my editor at Orbis Books, deserves special words of gratitude. My appreciation goes to all the good folks at Orbis Books who assisted in the production of this book.

Larry Hedges read the text twice and offered vital personal and writerly counsel. My own editors offered important contributions to this work: Greggory Moore, Heather Lee Miller, and Charlotte Weber. And I extend my thanks to Gerardo Rodríguez J., news editor at *Diario de Juarez-Diario de El Paso*, for permission to reprint selected photographs. Susilio Nugroho assisted me with all computer woes, and Kristen Entringer edited my photographs. The photos are mine unless otherwise indicated.

I offer thanks to my brother priests: Chris Smith, Michael J. McKieran, Doug Cook, Bao Thai, Joseph Trong, Simon Kim, Alex Ha, Seamus Glynn, Quan Tran, Paul Vu, and Timothy Nguyen. Fergus Clark accompanied me on this journey.

Many others also kept me going: Willard Maletz, Nina Yosphe, Terrie and Susan St. Germain, Timothy Doering, Ricardo Mercado, Patty and Tom Rauch, Blase Villa, Sergio Paniagua, Noa Wagner, Elidia Rubalcaba, Berta Aragón, and Chad Fults. Last, my thanks to the staff at Holy Family Cathedral.

Preface

My devotion to the missing and dead women of Juárez began unexpectedly. At the breakfast table one morning back in 1993 I read the briefest of newspaper accounts reporting on the discovery of what would be merely the first of the hundreds of women's bodies that would be found in the desert on the outskirts of Ciudad Juárez in northern Mexico. In that instant my life changed. During the years that followed I tracked the various developments in northern Mexico—the passage of NAFTA, the rise of the *maquiladoras,* the violence of the drug cartels—that contributed to the escalating count of the missing and the murdered. In 2004 I received grants from Chapman University that allowed me to begin my formal research into the topic with the first of many visits to El Paso and Juárez.

My family, friends, academic colleagues, and brother priests all advised against such dangerous research. My bishop cautioned me three times to stop this work (though later he would come to fully support my effort). Interviewees on the border and beyond who had firsthand knowledge of the immediate dangers involved repeated these admonitions. Once, while interviewing a U.S. congresswoman familiar with the border deaths, I was bluntly advised, "No good can come of this project. I am telling you that you need to stop this right now."

But no warnings could have prepared me for the reality of what I learned. My initial field research left me dumbfounded, unable to sleep, haunted by the horror from which I could not turn away. I was compelled to make some sense of such senseless brutality and suffering.

As the years passed the handful of dead women multiplied into hundreds, and consideration of the meaning of their suffering evolved into my life's work. In this book, as a priest and a theologian, I ask fundamental questions about the suffering of the innocent. I have found that to probe this issue is to share Job's spiritual journey, the man the scriptures tell us underwent a lengthy trial of suffering that forged in him a manner of loving God unconditionally, a love "indifferent" to whether God's plans accorded with his. Only when pushed to extremity in his suffering does Job go so far as to demand an audience so that God might explain that which has befallen Job, God's ever faithful servant. God's response, though, is not what Job imagined.

At the risk of overstretching the analogy, in my demand for answers I have not found what I expected either. And each week when I learn of more victims in the Juárez desert, I hear an urgent echo of Job's outcry, an echo that is amplified by the apparent lack of interest on either side of the border and a chronic failure to stop the killings.

Why would anyone study the butchering of hundreds of women? In my case the explanation begins in childhood. When I was about ten years old, I saw a photograph in *Maryknoll Magazine* that served as one of my inspirations to the priesthood. After nearly fifty years my memory of the photo remains fresh: a young man with his shirt open, soaked in what appears to be mud, holds a limp child in his arms. Surrounding the man are a few villagers of Asian extraction; in the background is lush green foliage. The caption explains the snapshot: the child had fallen into the village latrine and drowned. No family member or villager dared enter the pit to recover the child's body; only the Maryknoll priest braved such a task.

As a child it was difficult for me to comprehend what the photo documented. Growing up in the mid 1960s, I had never seen a priest who was not donned in silk and lace for the holy mass or dressed in black with a white Roman collar, even at parish picnics or fiestas. Reconciling the image of this young, athletic man in jeans with his role as a priest was difficult enough, even before I came to comprehend that what dripped from him head to toe was not mud but human excrement.

Still, I am certain that the photo would have slipped from memory but for a final detail offered in the caption: the priest had not entered the latrine to save the child from drowning—as I first presumed—but to retrieve his dead body. Care of the dead speaks to the sacredness of human dignity, especially when catastrophe seemingly ravages that dignity with utter randomness. While Mother Teresa ministered to the sick and the dying, this anonymous priest in a certain sense went further, risking his life for a child who was already beyond rescue. His action restored dignity to the dead, giving meaning to a seemingly senseless event and exemplifying both corporal and spiritual works of mercy: burying the dead and comforting the afflicted.

In popular Christian renditions the gospel figure of the good shepherd is most often depicted with groomed locks and graceful flowing garment caressing a hapless snowy-white lamb (Lk 15:1–7; Jn 10:1–15). But when I hear the Johannine text, the image that comes to my mind is of that missionary priest, leaving the other ninety-nine sheep to descend into a pool of excrement and retrieve the corpse of a child.

The theological methodology I employ in this work reflects another of my interests, that of spiritual theology. This manner of theologizing is grounded in a living experience of the Divine. Therefore, with regard to the feminicides, an appreciation of a context that is both sociopolitical and economic is indispensable as I ask about God's relationship to the particular causes of human suffering, as well as the presence of the Divine in such suffering. Such inquiry has been a difficult process, not only because the atrocities are so horrific and numerous and their cruelty so extreme but also because the Divinity's relationship to these woman-killings—and all senseless human suffering—is shrouded in mystery.

Mystery governs all theological inquiry, but when innocent blood is shed, mystery gives rise to confusion, which can lead to anguish, rebellion, and even a descent into despair and disbelief. What is God's relationship to the torture, rape, murder, and dismemberment of hundreds of young women? These darkest of human experiences present the most challenging of questions; we must not turn away from them but instead try to find in them some theological sense. If a theology and a faith cannot respond comprehensively and compassionately, then it is a sham theology, a sham faith. As St. Paul proclaims, "And if Christ has not been raised, our preaching is void of content and your faith is empty, too" (1 Cor 15:14).

The documentation of the murders in Juárez is an essential act of bearing witness. My field research and photographs serve as evidence of a horror that both the perpetrators and many with political and economic interest in northern Mexico would rather go undocumented. But document it we must, lest the women be forgotten. In so doing we also preserve a vital part of our own humanity.

Of the thousands of photographs I have taken in the course of my research, only a handful appear in this work. Most were snapped in haste, sometimes with a soldier or policeman pointing a machine gun at me in an attempt to prohibit me from taking pictures. Rarely was there time to compose the "best" shot. These images, as well as hundreds of others from the posters of missing women and from the work of photo journalists like Jaime Bailleres,[1] have proven foundational to my theological reflection. In seeking to comprehend them, I have been profoundly influenced by the Catholic Church's rich history of art and iconography, a tradition whose central subject is the passion of Christ.

Additionally, the writings of Roland Barthes and Susan Sontag have influenced on my taking, understanding, and use of the photographic image.[2] These thinkers, along with friend and essayist Richard Rodriguez, have led me to view the pictures of the missing and murdered women of Juárez as a contemporary and living christological passion whose human drama is represented by the still image of the photograph.

Other reasons for my commitment to the dead women will become evident in the pages that follow. But I add here another childhood memory, one of anxiously waiting for my mother to return home from her shift at the Cox Toy Factory on Logan Street in Santa Ana, California. For years as an adult I passed that old structure several times a week, and each time I did so I thought of my mother, who, like so many of the dead women of Juárez, worked as an assembly-line laborer. Largely because of her efforts I am now privileged to serve as a priest and university professor and to be in the position to write about this ongoing desert tragedy.

The silenced cries of the missing and dead women of Juárez reverberate for those who dare to listen. To engage their suffering is to sojourn with Job. This work extends an invitation to that passage.

Pink crosses. *This makeshift memorial is the site where eight women's remains were dumped. Some remains were identified and returned to their families for closure. More than a decade later, an unknown number of families of missing women are still waiting. These crosses were removed in February 2007.*

Introduction

What Remains?

My daughter's life as that of sheep or goat,
One victim from the thronging fleecy fold! . . .
That deed of his, I say, that stain and shame.
—CLYTEMNESTRA,
IN AESCHYLUS'S *AGAMEMNON*

INTRODUCTION: PINK CROSSES

I won't have much time. My eyes speedily survey the abandoned cotton field. It's about the size of a baseball green, scattered with dry brush and a few scrawny trees.

At my back is the busy intersection of Ejército National and Paseo de la Victoria located in southeastern Ciudad Juárez. On the lot's far side, an irrigation ditch with overgrown reeds cuts through its length. At its front, pink wooden crosses create a makeshift memorial to the eight women whose remains were dumped here in November 2001.[1] I start snapping photos; I'll study the pictures later—assuming the police or military guards don't take away my camera.

I hear city traffic in the background, but it's the silence of the dead that holds my attention. Grassroots women activists have painted hundreds of these pink crosses in Juárez—on the sides of buildings, on light posts, on the backs of newsstands, street signs, and telephone poles. For those who have eyes to see them, they are everywhere. For many, the crosses are unwanted reminders of a killing rampage. These activists paint the crosses as symbols of protest against both the violence itself and the failure of the Mexican political, law enforcement, and judicial systems to stop these murders.

I walk over to the crosses, each sun-faded marker standing approximately five-and-one-half feet tall. A victim's first name is painted on the horizontal bar of each: Brenda, Claudia Ivette, Lupita, Esmeralda, Barbara, Veronica, and Laura Berenice.[2] I also see one for a woman whose identity could not be established—a common occurrence because of a corpse's mutilation or decomposition. Women fitting this category are commonly known as *desconocidas*,[3] while women who have disappeared are *desaparecidas*. These terms have become all too familiar in Juárez, it seems, just as the perpetrators want it. By obscuring their whereabouts and even identities, it is easier to remove the victims from our thoughts. And the greater this distance, the more likely that their suffering will not touch us.

I try to figure out what happened here. The crosses stand about ten feet in front of the ditch. With a stone-and-cement bridge spanning it that is wide enough for pedestrians, the ditch is the most logical place to discard the bodies. Yet the nearest street is too far away for the killers to have hand-carried the corpses. They must have driven vehicles—most likely trucks—across the field and then tossed in the remains. There is no lighting, so under cover of darkness the task could be easily and secretly accomplished. Certainly, no one would have tried to stop the killers.

I allow the event to turn in my head; I am assaulted by the atrocity—exactly the effect I believe the killers intended.

Why leave the bodies in the middle of Ciudad Juárez? One possibility is "corpse messaging": using human bodies to send messages. As if a corpse is not message enough, words or phrases are often written on the body itself or on scraps of the dead person's clothing.[4] In this case, female bodies are used as billboards to announce the killers' reign, to demonstrate their power. As wolves mark and claim their territory with piss, so do these killers use women's corpses to stake their claim on all of Juárez. Terrorizing and intimidating the local population augments the killers' immunity. The corpses memorialized by the pink crosses are the ultimate warning to others to stay out of the way. The utter disregard for these women's bodies testifies to the depraved sickness of the killers. I wonder if perhaps the murderers got some bizarre sexual satisfaction from abusing the corpses.

The murderers' motivations and messages are distinct issues from what the women suffered prior to their death. The brutality to which they were subjected is harder for me to think about. I offer a silent prayer for the victims and bless this memorial ground.

Something catches my eye at the foot of a cross for Esmeralda. I bend down for a closer look: it is a burned-out candle in a glass votive featuring the image of Our Lady of Guadalupe, Mexico's beloved patroness, that lies in the dirt. Clearly, I am not the first to pray here. I can't help but recall that the Virgin vowed to Juan Diego that she came not to change the sufferings of her people but to share in them.

As I ponder this thought, head down, I hear the whirling blades of a helicopter in the distance. My time here is ended.

Quickly the sound grows louder. I lift my head to see the chopper whirl and then tilt right above me. From out of nowhere two soldiers rush toward me.

I turn and face them.

"*¡Manos arriba!*" the soldier on the left shouts. He does all the talking and both soldiers fix their machine guns on me, even though they are now only six feet away.

As commanded, I raise my hands. But instead of bullets the soldier fires questions at me: Am I a journalist? What is my name? From what country? Where is my identification?

Too many questions and demands at once. "I am not a journalist," I say.

"What are you doing here?"

"I've come to see and pay my respects to the dead women."

"Who are you?" I am silent.

"Who are you?" the soldier insists.

"*Soy sacredote*," I say calmly. "I am a priest."

The soldier questioning me tilts his head curiously, trying to take in my reply. The helicopter has moved on. There is a long silence as the two soldiers size me up. I stand six feet tall. I am middle aged, wearing jeans and a red t-shirt. An expensive Nikon camera hangs around my neck. The soldiers must also be considering my brown complexion, facial features, and jet-black hair. I am a Latino, but am I native Mexican? Finally the soldier doing the questioning mutters, "A pastor?"

"A father."

"*¿Cómo?*"

"*Padre*," I say. "A father—as in the Father, Son, and Holy Spirit."

My silly remark elicits smirks on both soldiers' faces. I see the tips of their machine guns slowly descend. Abruptly, the silent soldier raises his gun again, and a single word falls weakly from his mouth: "*¿Padre?*" he asks, as if just to make certain.

"*Sí,*" I say with a friendly smile. I lower my arms.

KILLINGS AND DISAPPEARANCES

Since 1993, at least 550 women and girls have been killed and more than 250 have disappeared from the border town of Juárez, Mexico, and the surrounding state of Chihuahua.[5] "Domestic violence" was listed as the official cause of approximately two-thirds of these murders. The second most common cause, accounting for about one-third of the total, is "targeted sexual violence."[6] The murders of many women in Juárez seem to fit this categorization. The victims are almost without fail between the ages of ten and thirty, of medium build, with shoulder-length hair, and from poor families. The striking similarities make it seem that they are not randomly chosen. Additionally, a ritualistic and depraved pattern exists to how these women were kidnapped, bound and gagged, tortured, and ultimately killed. Evidence shows repeated sexual violation. Many of the bodies display cut marks above the buttocks. Often the women's nipples have been bitten off. Some have their clitoris and labia sliced away with a knife. A number of the bodies are burned. Sometimes, only mutilated remains are found. Most often, these bodies are hidden carelessly in the desert sands. But even more disturbing are the displays of corpses in public places such as street intersections. Apparently, the killers believe that exploiting the women's bodies in such a way demonstrates their own power and immunity from the law.

A long, complex, and frustrating history lies behind such arrogance. Local, national, and international investigators have attempted to apprehend the perpetrators and hold them accountable for their crimes. The United Nations and Amnesty International, as well as journalists and academics, have conducted independent investigations. Yet few of the perpetrators have been caught and prosecuted. And there has been no comprehensive explanation for the deaths and disappearances. Nor has there been a resolution.[7]

FEMINICIDE

In the last fifteen years the evolution of terminology regarding the woman-killing in Northern Mexico reflects an increasing understanding of the nature of these murders.[8] Through the mid-1990s the killings were commonly referred to as the *maquiladora* murders, a simple reference to the fact that factory *(maquiladora)* workers represented a significant portion of the victims. But eventually it became apparent that the victims were not only *maquiladora* workers but lower- and middle-class women from various walks of life, including students and domestic workers. We also know that the murders extend beyond Ciudad Juárez to the whole of the border state of Chihuahua. In recent years the term favored by scholars is *femicide*.[9] The term denotes the murder of females by males because of the victims' gender; it is an act intended to bolster male dominance by rendering women chronically and profoundly unsafe.

In the past five years many scholars have come to feel that *femicide* is too narrow a determination for the Juárez woman-killing, given the multifarious reasons for the murders and the complex chain of culpability. Thus *feminicide* is increasingly employed as the more comprehensive term.[10]

Feminicide is a word loaded with sociological and political significance.[11] It not only connotes the murders of women by men because of the victims' gender but also implies state responsibility for the murders, whether through the actual commission of killings, toleration of the perpetrators' acts of violence, or failure to ensure the safety of its female citizens. To put it another way, the term *feminicide* advances the idea that the state and judicial structures normalize misogyny.

The European Parliament emphasizes these points when defining *feminicide,* focusing on the following:

- its relation to sexual and domestic violence;
- the lack of an effective official response to gender-based violence;
- impunity for the perpetrators;
- extreme brutality, usually of a sexual nature; and
- the large number of killings.[12]

Given this developing terminology and its clarification in this work, I refer to the approximately five hundred killings and three hundred abductions in Northern Mexico over the last two decades as the Juárez-Chihuahua feminicides.

ORGANIZATION AND APPROACH[13]

What remains in the devastating wake of the Juárez-Chihuahua feminicides? The many pressing and complex questions include: Why are the women being killed? Who commit these atrocious acts? Why have the killings continued for nearly two decades without any significant action to stop them? What political, economic, and social factors are in play at the U.S.–Mexico border, of which the feminicides are just one consequence?

Yet beyond these practical questions two enduring and ineffable mysteries remain. First, there is the mystery of human suffering radically manifested in the butchered bodies of hundreds of women. This suffering also encompasses the grieving of family, friends, and communities, as well as of all those who earnestly try to make sense of these killings. They must all face the suffering of anger, shock, disbelief, and confusion. In this work I consider the meaning of the senseless suffering of these women, and while I hope to arrive at an appropriate response to this tragedy, there will always be something unexplainable about human pain—especially senseless suffering. This truism leads to the second ineffable mystery. I sustain throughout this work the firm belief in God as omnipotent, omnipresent, and omnibenevolent. The challenge, then, is how to reconcile the human suffering of Juárez and God's divine attributes.

In this book I focus on the three perennial and universal questions the feminicides raise about all human suffering and the mercy of God: (1) What is the meaning and purpose of these women's suffering? (2) What is God's relationship to this suffering in Juárez? and (3) What are appropriate and inappropriate responses to pain, especially senseless suffering? These three questions are also salient to each of us, because when tragedy strikes our lives, we cannot help but question: Why is this happening to me? What have I done to incur God's punishment? What can I do to regain God's favor so as to alleviate my suffering?

In this, the feminicides are not unique. We question the suffering present in the brutality of war, in the oppression of the poor, and in disease and hunger. But if part of being human is to suffer, so too is the search for explanation and relief. Suffering is an irritant that yearns for a balm. In the theological tradition, consideration of God's relation to human suffering is called the *theodical problem*. If God is understood as all powerful, all knowing, and all good, then we must ask how the Divinity can allow such suffering to occur. Thus we enter into the conundrum of attempting to understand human suffering in a way that preserves God's integrity. This creates a related methodological issue—the primary focus becoming the general and abstract problem of reconciling this divine integrity. Approaching this preoccupation can never capture the concrete reality of individual suffering.

Traditional theological consideration of the missing and dead women reduces their suffering to a metaphysical problem and views the motivations for the killings as ancillary. With such methodology the challenge to formulate appropriate and up-to-date responses cannot occur, because the appropriate questions are never asked. A grossly insensitive response to the humanity of feminicide victims is the costly price of such theorizing.

In examining the feminicides I consider the rich tradition of theodical teachings with respect to past and present beliefs, attitudes, and actions regarding suffering, deconstructing them inasmuch as they have proven unhelpful or even unhealthy, while applying them where they prove helpful. My primary approach is to consider the particular suffering of the missing and murdered women and their survivors.[14] My ultimate goal is to arrive at a theologically comprehensive and humane way of coming to grips with the particular sufferings of the victims of the feminicides and to gain a better understanding of our own suffering. One criterion for the validity of a theological response to suffering is its applicability to the particular. That is, can a given theological response provide a viable source of consolation to the relatives, friends, and communities of the missing and dead women? And so, in this book I search for a theology of suffering that offers a comprehensive and compassionate response to the sufferings in and around Juárez.

A THEOLOGICAL EVENT

The social sciences have examined the Juárez feminicides as a historical and cultural phenomenon.[15] But secular understandings cannot adequately respond to the devastation of this human tragedy and the theodical questions it poses. We must also understand the feminicides as a theological event.

The English word *event* is derived from the Latin *evenire*, which comes from the suffix *e* meaning "out" and root verb *venire* meaning "to come." Thus, *event* can be read as meaning "to come out of."[16] Theologically, a cultural occurrence becomes an event when God comes out of that occurrence and makes a claim on one's whole person. The Juárez-Chihuahua feminicides include the secular and historical aspects of this phenomenon, but the secular disciplines that attempt to make some sense out of these killings do not. Understanding the feminicides as a theological event radically alters our understanding of them and extends our perspective beyond the killings themselves to ethical considerations of our complicity and response to these murders. It also helps us recognize both the dehumanization inherent in these deaths and an appreciation of each woman's human dignity, along with the plight of each woman's family, friends, and local communities—all victims of each tragedy. In truth, every one of us is in some way affected. Those of us who are changed enough by the feminicides to recognize this fact will decide to take appropriate action to help end these deaths.

Considering the feminicides as a theological event helps us examine what is revealed about humanness and the Divinity by way of human suffering. The extension of mere divine sympathy to the suffering women seems an inadequate divine response. From a theological perspective, rather, we should understand God as being in solidarity with these women—to the point that we realize that if the women make a claim on us, God is also making a claim on us.

Theorizing the feminicides as a theological event extends an invitation for us to participate in the form of a call-and-response dialectic. We are asked to have the courage to recognize what is occurring in Juárez and the violence and horror to which these women have been subjected. Then we face the inevitable choice: either turn away from the event or allow it to make a claim on us, thereby becoming a participant. If we choose the latter, it becomes incumbent upon us to take action to stop the suffering. And if we become participants, along with the survivors of the horror left to carry on in its wake, we share in the struggle to make sense of the event, wrestling with God's relation to this human suffering. Our participation in the call-and-response dialectic is operative in direct proportion to our positive response to engage the woman-killings.

INTERPRETIVE DISCOURSES

In consideration of the feminicides as a theological event I utilize several methodologies. Theological discourse dominates the major portion of this presentation. Yet journalists, academicians, humanitarians, and artists have also all contributed to the discourse on the killings, and their views are essential to formulating a comprehensive theological response. And so, this book cannot but be an interdisciplinary presentation. To present their work I employ what sociologist Rosa Linda Fregoso calls "interpretive discourses."[17] These discourses represent important research and reflection of the social sciences that assist in understanding the causative landscape of the feminicides.[18] They are interpretative because they offer a particular perspective on what is occurring in Juárez, although, as we shall see, not all these discourses are in accord. Therefore, while each discourse operates independently, all are interrelated, and collectively these discourses give us an overall view of these massive killings. For example, Chapter 1 presents a discourse on globalization and the consequences of the economic changes on the border community. Included is a treatment of narcotrafficking, which, despite being an illegal industry, is a Mexican institution of the highest order. Chapter 2 presents a discourse on morals and culture that reviews social factors related to the feminicides. Chapter 3 presents a narrative of the González-Flores family, a member of which was the victim of targeted sexual violence. This chapter also initiates our theological consideration of the Juárez-Chihuahua feminicides by introducing theological understandings of affliction and alienation.

NARRATIVE THEOLOGY

An essential tool at work in the theological discourse of this work is narrative theology. Narratives appear at the beginning of each chapter, and in accord with the methodology of this work, they offer particular examples of the realities of Juárez and specific missing or murdered women. These narratives are also immediately related to the understanding of the Juárez-Chihuahua feminicides as a theological event. God is revealing something important in Juárez—women's suffering—that demands our attention. And so these narratives assist us in our search for God and in making sense out of this human suffering.

When reading these narratives, we must keep two points in mind. First, we should not lose sight of the fact that ultimately every Christian narrative is a retelling of the mystery of death and resurrection of Jesus Christ. With this in view, it can be said that these narratives are a retelling of this pivotal Christian event as embodied by the circumstances and persons in Juárez. Next, it should be understood that at their core these narratives are stories of hope. Christians believe the resurrection to be the pinnacle of the Christian story. Finding hope is necessary to facing the gruesome realities of the feminicides. I extend these narratives to the victims' survivors, to all who follow the unfolding drama in Juárez, and to all who struggle to make sense of the pain in our lives.

PART I

THE EVENT

Serial killings fuel curiosity. A host of theories has accumulated over the years as to the identity of the Juárez-Chihuahua murderers and the reasons for their crimes. Initial conjecture as to their motivation has ranged from an international organ-harvesting ring to human sacrifices of satanic cults, as well as the possibility of there being single or multiple American serial killers crossing to the South to find victims and then returning to safety in the North.

Spurred by escalating public and international outcry, the Mexican authorities sought to bring a quick resolution to these feminicides, seemingly by seizing the nearest possible suspects. In 1995 an Egyptian national named Abdul Latif Sharif was arrested, charged, and convicted of a single murder. Many breathed a sigh of relief because a presumed serial killer was behind bars. Then more women were killed. Speculation rose that Sharif was somehow directing others from his jail cell to continue the killings.

In the years that followed, a series of arrests was made. In 1996 authorities apprehended several members of Los Rebelds, a Juárez street gang. In 1999, after a young woman made accusations against a bus driver, the authorities arrested the bus drivers of the routes between the *maquiladoras* and the *colonias*. In 2001 two men, García Uribe and Gonzáles Meze, were arrested for the murder of eight victims.

But these arrests for specific murders did not stop the killings, and the border community remained terrorized. Therefore, a broader thesis must be invoked to explain the phenomenon. I contend that these murders are the consequence of a maelstrom of collective causes. The ambiguity and complexity of these killings, along with the dark intrigue of a murder mystery—a whodunit—cannot sidetrack us from the particular causes in play.

Prior to considering these factors and parties as presented in the various interpretative discourses, I make one essential point: The immediate violence against these missing and dead women is the immense responsibility of some men in Juárez and the surrounding locals. Unleashing some primitive and savage internal inclinations, these men exercised their free will to commit these deeds to vent their destructive rage at women who were innocent and vulnerable. Their exigent cruelty has been repeated over again hundreds of times, creating and perpetuating a realm of human suffering for which, I believe, they will ultimately be held responsible.

On the watch. *Since 2009, five thousand federal police officers and the same number of Mexican Army soldiers have been patrolling the streets of Juárez. Despite their efforts the number of missing and murdered women, as well as the illegal narco-related violence, continues to escalate.*

1

Juárez

Juárez, where drugs move, people die, bribes grace palms.

—Charles Bowden[1]

BORDER WALK, PENTECOST SUNDAY, JUNE 2011

Something irksome but unstoppable happens every time I leave El Paso for Juárez. As I mount the pedestrian walkway on the El Puente Santa Fe, in my head Marty Robbins is belting out his cowboy ballad "El Paso." El Puente's five-lane highway is an avenue for thousands who cross daily into the United States. On any given day it may require hours in the searing heat to reach the U.S. border station, followed by what can be a long border-check process. Today, a Sunday at 2:00 p.m., the bridge is a parking lot.

Passengers on the bridge are both entertained and annoyed by scurrying Mexican vendors who hawk everything from black-velvet renditions of Our Lady of Guadalupe to knock-off designer t-shirts. I dawdle and take in this border circus. A determined old cowboy with a wide-brimmed hat pushes past me. When I get to the middle of the bridge, I am a straddler, neither here nor there, suspended, in a no-man's land between two countries.

The U.S.–Mexican border is an in-between space of countless interpretations. But most area residents agree that the border is better understood not as a line but as a region that extends twenty miles on either side.

Overhead, just twenty-five feet from each other, wave each nation's flag. Below is the muddy Rio Grande, twenty yards wide and flowing briskly through its concrete waterway. The river is the divide between the United States and Mexico, though the desert heat can reduce this "grand river" to a measly trickle.

On my right I can trace the modest El Paso skyline, a collection of about twenty mid-sized skyscrapers. Behind the buildings rises Franklin Mountain, adorned with a huge five-point star that illuminates at night. On my left is Ciudad Juárez, a mass of low structures that ascend with the gently rising curvature of the land until the city stops suddenly at the base of the El Cerro Bola mountain range (so named because of the bowl-like shape of its center peak).

I can also see El Mirador (the lookout), a spot in the mountains to enjoy the best view of Juárez and also to see El Paso well enough to glimpse part of Franklin Mountain's Texas Star. El Mirador was once a popular getaway for lovers, but it is now known for the violence that occurs there. Two days from now, while I'm taking photographs of the city, four people will be gunned down.

When you take in the vista, you see a single valley divided into sister cities by an invisible, human-fabricated line. Some commentators refer to this area as a *borderplex*,[2] a term referring to any one of fourteen interlocked U.S.–Mexican border cities. El Paso-Juárez's combined population of more than two million residents makes this the second-most-populous borderplex.[3]

Many on the Mexican side see crossing that line as the promise of a new life. Meanwhile, U.S. business investors hold daytime business meetings in five-star restaurants in Juárez, a city whose *maquiladoras* generate huge profits. Nights are spent in first-class hotels.

Ultimately, however, the border is an arbitrary determination. Politicians, academics, writers, and artists all posit theories about this peripheral space.[4] Gloria Anzaldúa, whose border descriptions helped reformulate contemporary notions of what the border is, refers to this space as "two worlds merging to form a third country—a border culture." She calls the border itself "*una herida abierta*—an open wound . . . where the Third World grates against the First and bleeds."[5]

On the bridge I notice three U.S. border guards sitting in a shady spot, balancing their weight on the metal handrails, feet off the ground. They chat with one another, toothpicks dangling from their mouths, as they keep lazy eyes on the passing foot traffic. Farther down the bridge I pass three Mexican border guards feebly managing their weighty machine guns, weary from the heat.

Despite the border guards' relaxed deportment, combined U.S.–Mexico efforts to halt the drug cartels' illegal activities have made this line between two lands one of the world's most militarized peacetime borders.[6] Narcotraffickers make lucrative border crossings daily. A single stash of drugs smuggled into the United States can mean cash profits of millions of dollars.

I descend the Mexican side of the bridge, toss the required coins into a metal box, go through the turnstile, pass three utterly disinterested border guards, and land on Avenida Juárez. The avenida's namesake is "Mexico's Abraham Lincoln," the first indigenous national to serve as president, which he did for a remarkable five terms. Despite the honorific, this is one of the most hazardous streets on the globe. Having arrived in the infamous Ciudad Juárez, I take a moment to look back at El Paso, sometimes referred to as a "miracle" because of its very low crime rate among U.S. cities. Ciudad Juárez is the undisputed "murder capital of the world."[7]

I am struck by how different the avenida was six years ago, when Juárez was still a boomtown and a model industrial city for all of Mexico.[8] During Prohibition, Juárez had solidified its infamy as an American watering hole, and the Avenida Juárez, just a hop over the bridge, was the center of action. For decades the avenida's ill repute was an enticement for tourists, who made it their adult playground. Everything illegal in the United States was easily accessible there: liquor, prostitution, narcotics on every street corner. Additionally, there were fantastic shopping bargains. No wonder day-trippers packed into the avenida's abundant bars, restaurants, and stores—especially at night.

But at 3:00 p.m. on this Sunday, with only moderate June heat for this area, only a few cars traverse the stone-inlayed street, so few that I can see all the way down the mile-long avenida. Only a few locals appear, but no tourists anywhere. There's no real need to ask why. The previous night an atrocious slaying occurred in the city: nine people were killed, execution style. But as monstrous and shocking as this violence is, narco-related happenings have become commonplace in Ciudad Juárez. No wonder tourism is just another of the city's formerly thriving industries gone bust.

As I continue my walk, I see that the most famous tourist destination in Juárez has somehow survived. The Kentucky Club Bar and Grill is one of two or three Mexican bars that lay claim to the invention of the margarita. Established in the 1920s, the Kentucky Club immediately became a popular spot, thriving throughout Prohibition. Even as recently as a few years ago the Kentucky Club was a "must have a drink there" tourist stop. But today I can see only a lone patron, a local, balancing himself on a barstool, head nodding.

A detour down a random side street reveals two-story structures that once housed prosperous businesses now missing windows like knocked-out teeth, their unrepaired stucco crumbling to expose brick foundations. At the end of the street an entire city block once packed with bars and clubs has been bulldozed, the now-vacant lot another testimony to the border district's demise.

Back on Avenida Juárez a Mexican boy no older than seven dashes up to me with a green wooden box. "*¡Señor! ¡Señor!* Shoeshine?"

When President Felipe Calderón assumed office in 2006, he took the offensive against the narcos. Many blame him for the forty thousand persons killed in drug-related violence since then; eight thousand of them were slain here in Juárez.[9] Calderón put the army and federal police on the streets of Mexico, effectively making the entire country—Juárez, in particular—a war zone. Now day and night, soldiers and police patrol Juárez streets in open vehicles displaying mounted machine guns, a show of force that keeps an already uneasy populace in a constant state of fear.

In Juárez, the Sinaloa-Sonora and Juárez cartels are battling for control of the city, which is the access corridor to the U.S. narcotics market. Violence can erupt anywhere. In fact, the best districts and finest restaurants are often arenas for bloodshed. And since much of the violence in Juárez is random, everyone is at risk.[10]

"*¡Señor!* Shoeshine?" the boy persists.

More than a decade ago, Charles Bowden entitled his prophetic work, *Juárez: The Laboratory of Our Future*. Now, this future has arrived, and it is more dystopian than anyone could have predicted. The murder rate in Juárez has risen from 300 to the 3,951 recorded in 2010. According to Al Jazeera, "In Juárez there is a trail of blood that . . . can be followed day by day, hour by hour."[11]

"*¿Cómo te llames?*" I ask the boy.

"*Renato, señor.* Shoeshine?"

Renato is one of the lucky kids. At least he's employed, if only for a few cents a job. And he's got a work ethic.

Just one of the devastating consequences of the thousands of drug-related deaths is an entire generation of parentless children.

As a twisted result, it is often not teachers, businessmen, or even sports heroes and movie stars who serve as inspiration for these lost youths; they want to be *sicarios*, assassins. Many Mexican youths would rather burn up their adolescence as narcokillers, indulging in a few years of unimaginable luxury and excitement before dying young, rather than live a long life as a slave to poverty.

"*¿Por favor, señor?* Shoeshine?"

I offer Renato some coins, but skip the shine. "*Muchas gracias, señor*," he says, then dashes after another possible customer.

Across the street, I see *taxistas* waiting with open car doors in front of the Nuevo Sinaloa and Felix Bar. These dens are supposed narco hangouts, but I don't wait around to find out. Down the street most of the bars that once crowded this avenue have been replaced, ironically, by drugstores. Farmacias Benavides is one of the oldest and largest pharmacies, Mexico's equivalent to Walgreens. The name of the next drugstore tickles me: Farmacia del Dr. Descuento (Dr. Discount Pharmacy).

This changeover of business is telling. With tourism nearly extinguished, these pharmacies service border crossers willing to risk much in order to obtain medication that is three times cheaper than it is in the United States.

Avenida Juárez ends at Avenida 16 de Septiembre, an intersection dominated by a distinctly nineteenth-century, French-style, red-brick building that houses Juárez's Museum of History. This one-time customs house is where, in 1911, Mexican President Porfirio Díaz and U.S. President William Taft met. But today I have no interest in visiting this historical site. I am three-quarters of the way to my destination and must be there by 5:00 p.m.

While Avenida Juárez is devoid of traffic, 16 de Septiembre bustles with westbound transit. Buses expel foul exhaust, trucks of every size, fancy SUVs, and cars aplenty chart fanatically tangled routes, all without incident. I wait for the light to change, and then dash across the busy street. On the other side

I am assaulted by a newsstand spilling over with magazines featuring Justin Bieber and American Idol judge Steven Tyler. Is there no escape from American pop culture? But it is the scores of magazines with graphically explicit pictures of women that dominate the stand.

I make my way down the street and cross Calle Noche Triste, arriving at the Plaza de Armas. This mini-park is the traditional city center. Here, everyone fights for shade under the sparse trees. Men with baseball caps rest on the edge of the cement planters. In the center of the plaza a small, three-tiered fountain rains drops of water that thirsty pigeons immediately scoop up. Roberto Vesquez-Muñoz, a Sunday fixture in the plaza for the last two decades, preaches his usual call for political revolution.

In the Plaza de Armas posters displayed on light posts solicit information about missing women. The torn and battered posters are 14 by 9 inches in size. Atop each is the same announcement: *Ayúdanos A Localizarla* (Help us find her). On the first poster I meet Maria de la Luz Hernandez Cardona, who was eighteen years old when she disappeared on April 26, 2011—disappeared from the very neighborhood where I am standing. I want to reach out to the poster to offer Maria de la Luz some due respect, but the desert sun has bleached and dried the paper. The brittle poster would crumble at my touch, and Maria's plea would be lost.

The next poster is of Faviola Alejandra Ibarra Chavarria, who was only sixteen when she disappeared just the week before. On the opposite side of the plaza I see the remnants of more of the same. I take my camera out of my shoulder bag and discreetly make a photographic study of the posters.

Nearby, a diffident monument to the missing and dead women is almost lost under the shadow of the trees. A brown metal sign offers this counsel, which in translation reads: "All of the children of the world should know: 'A woman is never hit, not even with a rose petal.'"

As I write this chapter, my photographs spread out in front of me, I recall Susan Sontag's words regarding the extraordinary power of a picture to expose human suffering: "When I looked at those photographs, something broke. Some limit had been reached, and not only that of horror; I felt irrevocably grieved, wounded, but a part of my feeling started to tighten; something went dead; something is still crying."[12]

On the same block as the plaza is the Cathedral of Our Lady of Guadalupe. From the plaza the cathedral appears to be a standard-sized house of worship. Yet when I ascend the two-dozen stone steps to a smaller, more secluded plaza and stand immediately in front of the grand façade, I am dwarfed by the architectural design.

When I enter, I find the congregation gathering for the evening Pentecost liturgy. The reverence and particular silence of this community always strikes me. There is no chatter when the parishioners greet each other, no handing out of bulletins, no pre-liturgy announcements, no hymn rehearsal. The congregation waits in stillness. The only movement is the silent entry of worshipers through three sets of double doors on the left side of the cathedral. Above these doors a slab-glass depiction of Our Lady of Guadalupe rises two stories, dominating the wall. In the afternoon sun this heavy, multicolored glass casts a thin blue blush over the waiting congregation. In a gentle awakening I realize that in my mind Marty Robbins's balladeering has been replaced by the raucous city traffic churning outside the cathedral's confines. However comforted I am by the congregational tranquility, as I attempt to join in the Pentecost prayer, I cannot help recalling the wraithlike pictures of the missing women staring at the other side of the cathedral walls, women who were from this neighborhood, part of this community—women now silenced. Most likely, the people in this congregation include their coworkers, friends, and grieving family members.

I notice that above the side doors, red cloth Pentecost banners announce: *Enviá Señor tu Espíritu*—Lord, send your Spirit. I ponder the Pentecost bloodbath of nine narco executions of the previous night. Indeed, red is the appropriate color for this day. Out of habit I begin a slow succession of exhalations, and I can feel myself beginning to surrender. In the midst of cacophony and quiet, I join the Juarensen community in our wait for the sacred breath of the Holy Spirit.

Without a grand procession or even an entrance hymn, a priest draped in scarlet appears in the sanctuary. "*El Señor este con vosotros*," he says.

"*Y tu espíritu*," the congregation responds in unison.

The Pentecost Liturgy commences.

NAFTA AND THE RISE OF THE *MAQUILADORAS*

The year 1993 marked both the ratification of the North American Free Trade Agreement (NAFTA) and an escalation in various drug-cartel operations. In response to U.S. authorities closing off Miami as the primary entry point for drugs from Colombia, the Mexican and Colombian cartels reached an accord to turn the Mexican border into the U.S. market gateway. That same year the corpses of women began to be discovered in the desert surrounding Ciudad Juárez. In some cases the killers had made no efforts to hide the bodies but had put them on display, sending a grisly message.

When NAFTA went into effect on January 1, 1994, it created a trilateral trade bloc among Canada, the United States, and Mexico. Tariffs were eliminated on over one-half of U.S. imports from Mexico and on over one-third of U.S. exports to Mexico. U.S. companies could now produce goods south of the border to take advantage of reduced taxes and abundant cheap labor. Within ten years all tariffs were eradicated (with the exception

of some U.S. agricultural exports to Mexico, which were eradicated fifteen years later).

The pros and cons of NAFTA are the subject of much debate.[13] North of the border investors raked in profits, while
average Americans benefited from lower prices on commercial
and agricultural goods. South of the border Mexico welcomed
the new industrialization brought by the new NAFTA channels
and with it the creation of much-needed jobs for low-income
individuals. As a result, manufactured goods became Mexico's
chief export. All told, NAFTA has built up economic muscle in
both the United States and Mexico—and so it is often described
as a "win-win" situation.[14]

But within a decade the negative effects of NAFTA became
all too obvious. According to the Mexican Solidarity Network,
"the working class on both sides of the border suffers declining
standards of living."[15] As we will see, feminicide is just one of
the dehumanizing consequences of NAFTA for Mexico and the
United States.

It is important to note the breadth of NAFTA's impact in
Mexico's border corridor and specifically in Ciudad Juárez. U.S.
border companies particularly prospered from NAFTA. Suppliers north of the border were able to cut shipping costs and
time by working to their southern flank in Mexico instead of
relying on the labor force in China, continuing to purchase from
U.S. suppliers but completing assembly in Mexico. As a result,
maquiladoras in Juárez multiplied and thrived. The impact of the
maquiladora factor becomes clear when one considers that prior
to the 2008 economic crisis, 25 percent of all trade between the
United States and Mexico crossed over the Juárez–El Paso border and that in 2006, the $55 billion generated by U.S.–Mexico
trade accounted for 18 percent of all U.S. trade.[16]

"The word Maquiladora comes from colonial Mexico, where
millers charged a 'maquila' for processing other people's grain."
Today, the same term applies to assembly plants for consumer

goods.[17] For example, components for cars are imported into Mexico, assembled in these plants, and then exported with minimal taxes.[18]

Before the 2008 economic crisis there were approximately thirty-one hundred *maquiladoras* in Mexico, employing over one million workers.[19] Ciudad Juárez had become Mexico's *maquila* capital, boasting more than three hundred factories, which in total employed 267,000 workers, over half of whom were women.[20] The net result is that women obtained more impact on the supply side of regional economy than ever before.

Delphi Automotive Systems, Siemens, Honeywell, RCA, General Electric, Levi Strauss, and Lennox are just a few of the familiar brand names that had assembly plants in Juárez. These *maquiladoras* are concentrated in two modern industrial parks. A list of the goods that are assembled or produced in Juárez reads like a tribute to U.S. consumerism: cars, computers, medical equipment, clothing, and agricultural products. For better or for worse, the economies of the United States and Mexico are now inextricably joined. Nowhere is this more apparent than Ciudad Juárez.

To illustrate the level of U.S. dependence on Mexican products, consider Johnson Control's *maquiladoras* in Juárez. Though best known for producing automotive parts, Johnson Control dominates the commercial air-conditioning industry, producing essential elements for most of the commercial air conditioners in the United States and many of those in Europe. At these *maquiladoras* most of the labor is performed by women.[21]

Family members in Juárez often seek employment in the same *maquiladora*, and some are able to form family teams.[22] With a stroke of luck, or perhaps a bribe, they may even obtain the same work shift, enabling family members to commute together. *Maquiladora* employees regularly work night shifts, and a typical bus trip to a *maquiladora* runs from one of the slum *colonias* located on the outskirts of Juárez to one of the modern business parks within the city—a trip involving several bus transfers. When family members travel together—especially when women are accompanied by male relatives— it reduces the chances that they will become crime victims. But most workers are not fortunate enough to enjoy this safety and support.

Since *maquiladora* jobs do not pay well—assembly-line workers usually make less than US$50 weekly[23]—it is nearly impossible to survive on a single salary, and so family members combine their wages. This is not to say that increased gainful employment for women has not afforded them a degree of societal influence and independence, but these gains come at a perilous price.

The fallout from the 2008 economic crisis changed the industrial profile of Juárez, and of Mexico as a whole. Increasingly, NAFTA's promises were exposed as empty. When U.S. manufactures faltered or failed, between 80,000 and 100,000 persons lost their jobs, leaving the city in a state of economic disaster. Even the present and most optimistic views estimate that there is 800 million square feet of empty *maquiladora* space and at least sixty thousand workers waiting in Juárez for employment. Juárez's bright economic star fell, though both investors and workers alike hope for a speedy recovery.[24]

LAS INVASIONES

Two massive movements of people in and out of Juárez regularly occur, each with its own effects on the city. One is the sixty thousand people per day who make their way across the four bridges that join Juárez and El Paso.[25] This back and forth, the busiest international border crossing on the planet, is driven primarily by commerce. Juárez is also a magnet for Mexicans living to the south.[26] Their main reason for moving to cities is economic necessity.[27] This interior migration from rural to urban centers has long taken place but has increased dramatically since NAFTA's implementation. Currently, more than 76 percent of Mexico's population lives in urban areas.

Ciudad Juárez is a striking example of this change. University of Texas political-science professor Kathleen Staudt calls Juárez "a city of migrants," noting that "the majority of them [are] poor."[28] Over the last two decades Juárez has experienced higher population growth than the state of Chihuahua and the country as a whole.[29] As of 2000, about 32 percent of Juárez's population was composed of Mexicans born outside Chihuahua. Staudt's findings indicate that only around 30 percent of the women residing in Juárez were born there.[30] It is ironic, therefore, to consider that the poetic epithet for the hundreds of women murdered in this area is *hijas de Juárez* (daughters of Juárez). The phrase alludes to initiation by blood and does not relate to the victims' actual place of origin.[31]

Staudt also finds a prevailing derogatory attitude toward the city's migrants[32]—which I have also found in my research there. On the streets of Juárez the daily arrival of masses of peoples is called *las invasiones*. Renato Asenio León, Roman Catholic bishop of Juárez, estimates that between 2004 and 2005, some 100,000 people came to Juárez from the state of Veracruz alone.[33] With more people arriving constantly, it is difficult to calculate the actual number of people living in Juárez.

The Mexican Constitution specifies that Mexican citizens can freely settle land that is unoccupied and without claim for more than five years. This is an open invitation for migrants to inhabit the desert region outside of Ciudad Juárez. Unplanned communities referred to as *colonias populares* (poor, working-class districts or neighborhoods) sporting names like Lote de Bravo and Anapra sprawl across this open desert. These are vast slums, often without running water, electricity, public transportation, or adequate police protection. Many of the bodies of the murdered women of Juárez have been found dumped on the outskirts of these *colonias*. The majority of *maquiladora* workers reside in, and commute from, these unplanned shantytowns.

Prior to the 2008 economic crisis, only one thing was certain within this complex mass of humanity: endless thousands of people searching for work provided the fresh, ready, and cheap labor supply requisite for the continuing growth of the *maquiladoras* in Juárez. And they were entering a territory where drug trafficking is a far bigger and more dangerous business than anything taking place under the auspices of NAFTA.

A new and no less dramatic mass migration is now occurring in Juárez, though in a telling shift of direction: people are fleeing Ciúdad Juárez. Since Calderón declared his war on drugs in 2006, an astounding 230,000 people have left the city. Those with the economic resources—approximately one-half of these people—have sought safety in El Paso. Thousands of others less fortunate have relocated within in search of neighborhoods that might provide better security, however unlikely that prospect. The 2008 crisis has been a resounding declaration to those who once dreamed of working and living in Juárez that the window of opportunity has actually become a deathtrap of narco-related violence and joblessness.

EL NARCOTRAFFICO

The United States is indisputably the world's largest consumer of illegal narcotics. Mexico is its main source of heroin, marijuana, and methamphetamines.[34] Additionally, 70 percent of all cocaine consumed in the United States, while produced in South America, enters the country through Mexico.[35] This is a shift from the 1980s, when most U.S. cocaine came from Colombia by way of the Caribbean, its primary entry point being Miami.[36] Once the U.S. government managed to close that corridor, the Colombian cartels looked to Mexico's relatively unguarded border.[37] To facilitate the new logistics of the cocaine trade, Mexican and Colombian cartels arrived at an accord: the Colombian cartels would export their narcotics to the Mexican cartels, who would in turn smuggle them into the United States through Ciudad Juárez.

The Mexican cartels were poised to undertake such a massive and profitable venture by the consolidation of smaller Mexican cartels, a phenomenon that occurred during the 1960s and 1970s. Four large oligopoly cartels emerged, adopting nicknames relating to their geographical locations: the Tijuana Cartel, the Sinaloa-Sonora Cartel, the Gulf Cartel, and the Juárez Cartel. Ironically, their consolidation resulted primarily as a necessary response to the U.S. War on Drugs policies and initiatives. Skilled drug lords mastered the relative balance of power between these oligopoly cartels necessary to sustain an efficient inter-cartel working relationship (which included keeping the cartel members from killing one another).[38]

Despite perennially increased efforts on both sides of the border to counter their expansion,[39] the cartels have proven themselves to be adaptive and resilient.[40] And even with a recent fracturing of the inter-cartel alliance and almost daily eruptions of border violence, insatiable U.S. demand makes the trade in illegal narcotics a $30 billion industry annually.[41] Why have these two great nations been unable to stop the cartels? Journalist Charles Bowden puts it bluntly: "Drugs are a business, one of the largest on the surface of the earth, and this business exists for two reasons: the products are so very, very good and the profits are so very, very high."[42] Tony Payan offers his perspective of how the narcotics trade affects life in Juárez: "Having hitched itself successfully to American patterns of consumption, including drug consumption, it has also become the one city where the crunch of the war on drugs and the worldwide financial crisis have had a very heavy impact. . . . Tens of thousands of young men roam the streets with little or no hope of obtaining a job, of receiving drug treatment, of escaping the cycle of violence."[43]

Concerns that Mexico would go the route of Colombia—often referred to as the "Colombianization of Mexico"[44]—in its escalating pattern of corruption and violence have proven well founded. Colombia, for example, is considered the "kidnapping capital of the world," and now kidnapping has become a common danger in Mexico.[45] The difference for the United States is that Colombia, for all its violence, corruption, and exportation of illegal narcotics, remains a distant South American entity. But Mexico is the United States' southern neighbor, sharing ties that extend far beyond a free-trade agreement.

Contrary to popular assumptions, the drug trade and the migration of undocumented aliens into the United States have little correlation. Only small-time cartels would risk using pedestrians to smuggle precious drugs, especially walking north across the desert.[46] Historically, the most common means of smuggling narcotics has been by cars, vans, and pickup trucks. Typically, contraband is stashed in a hidden compartment called a *clavo* (nail). Although *clavos* are still employed, over the years NAFTA has changed the way drug trade operates.[47] Nearly five million trucks cross the U.S.–Mexico border every year, carrying 70 percent of all U.S.–Mexico trade, worth an estimated $360 billion.[48] Between January and July 2008, nearly four thousand trucks crossed from Juárez to El Paso, bringing nearly $100 million worth of goods per month.[49] It is in trucks like these, packed with legal goods, that the Juárez Cartel leaders smuggle contraband from Mexico to major metropolises in the United States.[50] Financial limitations and time restraints allow law enforcement officials to inspect only a small percentage of the massive number of trucks that pass across the border. This situation has led some to argue that NAFTA has benefited no border industry more than the illicit drug trade. Former U.S.

Drug Enforcement Administration employee Phil Jordan called NAFTA "a deal made in narco-heaven."[51]

CORRUPTION: COLLUSION AND IMPUNITY

The Mexican government has a long history of corruption, which has resulted in public distrust of government officials and organizations. Corruption is a way of life in Mexico, extending from rigging elections to paying *mordidas* (bribes) to get out of minor traffic violations.

Over the past twenty years public distrust of Mexico's government has been exacerbated by *narcopolítica*, what Payan refers to as a tacit agreement between Mexican authorities and the cartels regarding the level of protection that government will offer a cartel—or at least the extent to which the government will look the other way.[52] According to Secretary Eduardo Romero, head of the anticorruption effort under former President Vicente Fox, "impunity is what most influences the perception of civil society."[53] This impunity legitimizes violence.

Since the cartels possess a seemingly infinite reservoir of cash for bribes, corruption finds fertile ground in a government where weak institutions lack transparency and oversight.[54] Extensive investigation and documentation by groups such as Amnesty International and the United Nations, for example, confirm the deficiency of the investigations into murders related to narcotrafficking.[55] Additionally, the international media have made a growing number of accusations of narcotrafficking collusion by government officials.[56] Because of the increasing inter-cartel violence of recent years, police and military have been the subject of increased government and media scrutiny. In June 2007 corruption was found to be so prevalent that President Calderón replaced all of the country's federal police chiefs in one fell swoop.[57] Organized crime is so widespread that it has undermined the very rule of law and respect for basic human rights.[58] And Juárez, as a hub of narcotics smuggling, is notorious for such corruption.[59] In 2011 Mexican statistics show that 95 percent of murders presumed to involve organized crime were never investigated by Mexican authorities; and of those cases that make it to trial, no more than 2 percent result in sentencing.[60]

CONCLUSION

Like strange bedfellows, El Paso and Ciudad Juárez embrace at the Rio Grande in a pulsating, symbiotic enterprise of commerce, politics, and cultural exchange. Daily, thousands of people cross back and forth in an endless stream between these sister cities. Yet in many ways these two wedded cities remain divergent and seemingly detached. For example, on the north side of the border, El Paso shines as the safest city in the United States, whereas to the south, Juárez mars Mexico as the murder capital of the world.

After NAFTA's implementation in 1994, industry boomed in Juárez, drawing thousands upon thousands of workers from rural Mexico to the *maquiladoras.* Yet since the 2008 recession, nearly 300,000 persons with means have left the border metropolis, while most Juarenses ensnared by poverty remain unemployed in the death trap of a city plagued by daily bloodbaths. The Mexican drug cartels, once a secret underworld enterprise, have now seized control of Juárez with blatant displays of ever-escalating violence. No end to the mayhem is in sight.

The brutal killing of women went unnoticed until 1993, when the unearthing of the skeletal remains of women sounded an alarm that could no longer escape national and international attention. In the following two decades a maelstrom of change occurred in Juárez, initiated by an economic rise that most recently turned into industrial disaster. Throughout, the murders have been constant, with hundreds of instances of domestic and targeted sexual violence. Very few of these cases were subject either to substantive investigation or to prosecution. This apparent disinterest in justice points to a Mexican sociopolitical structure rife with corruption and tacit rapport with the ruling narcotraffickers. Posters soliciting information about the hundreds of missing women have become so commonplace in Juárez that such solicitations hardly turn pedestrians' heads.

The United States acknowledges but takes little responsibility for the fact that its rampant illegal narcotic consumption fuels the drug wars raging in Mexico. These battles, though just a stone's throw away from the border, are still sufficiently distant for the U.S. mainstream consciousness to recognize that the illegal narcotic trade is a mutual problem with Mexico—so too the corruption. Nor have U.S. industrial investors demonstrated any significant accountability for the safety of the women they employ—and endanger.

Why do so many women die in Northern Mexico? How could these kidnappings and killings go on for nearly twenty years without comprehensive action to stop them? How do we begin to make sense out of the human pain palpable on any Juárez city street? Where do we search for God in the border metropolis? Here, I offer an interpretive discourse on Juárez's corruption and violence as the primary causes of the human suffering of all Juarenses. This serves as the background for our consideration of the woman-killing and the theological reflection on the meaning and response to suffering.

Coral Arrieta Medina

Coral Arrieta Medina. Medina, age seventeen, was found on March 14, 2005, in an area of Juárez known as Lote de Bravo, where eighteen other victims had been found in previous years. This photo appeared on March 17 in the local newspaper El Diario de Juárez. *No killer has been found, but according to authorities, "the case is under investigation."*

2

What Is Killing the Women?

*¡Yo se quienes estan matando las mu-
jeres! ¡Yo se!
(I know who's killing the women! I
know!)*

—SHOUTS HEARD ON A JUÁREZ STREET CORNER

CORAL ARRIETA MEDINA,
WEDNESDAY, MARCH 17, 2005

I approach a newsstand on Avenida 16 de Septiembre in
Ciudad Juárez. It's just a large metal box that opens up to the
sidewalk with the back of the stand facing the avenue. I look
for painted pink crosses on the stand, but there are only dents
and chipped green paint. At the stand's base lie fresh stacks of
El Diario, the local newspaper. I pick up today's edition, toss
the attendant a few coins, and step away a few feet to read the
headline: "The Murdered Woman Was a Minor."[1]

The body of seventeen-year-old Coral Arrieta Medina was
found in an empty lot on the outskirts of the city where eighteen
other victims had been found within the last year. She was the
eighth found in 2005 and the second in the past three days. She
had been reported as a *desaparecida* five days earlier. Her body
was found partially clothed. Originally from Veracruz, Coral had
migrated to Juárez and had been a university student studying

computer science while holding down employment in a *maqui-laldora*. The autopsy revealed she had been sexually molested; the cause of death was asphyxiation by strangulation. Her body was discovered approximately twenty-four hours after her death.

I study Coral's picture. It is a standard headshot for a student ID card. She is an attractive young woman with dark hair, her brown complexion unobscured by makeup. She wears a white-collared blouse and grayish-blue jumper—most likely a school uniform. Her tapered eyebrows arch gracefully high. Her large, brown eyes seem intense with concentration. She appears a serious young woman; her full lips are unsmiling.

I wonder how many commutes Coral made each day, and at what hours. Fear was most likely her unwanted companion on these trips. I stare at her picture until its colored newspaper dots seem to dance in midair.

When I lift my head, the array of magazines on the newsstand grabs my attention: *Latina*, *Hispana*, *Star*, *TV Nota*, even a couple of Daisy Duck comic books. But it is an arsenal of pornography that dominates the stand. I look down at Coral's photo on the front page of the stack of newspapers and see her flanked by a phalanx of carnal, graphic shots of women. Every row of the newsstand, corner to corner, top to bottom, is packed with pornography.

Later that week I am in the southernmost point of Juárez, where the city ends and the open desert begins. I've heard Juarenses speak in whispers about what goes on here. To my right are shacks constructed of crates, cardboard, plywood, tin, old doors, and whatever else could be found. Clotheslines strung between the rows of hovels hold garments that sway in the desert wind. Dust is ubiquitous; clean clothes are a luxury. Many residences do not have running water.

Three men talk while sitting on upside-down plastic contain-ers. Power lines randomly stretch from poles to concrete-and-brick one-room homes, though clearly not all have electricity. To my left is a wide-open desert road strewn with old tires, cans, scrub brush, and every imaginable kind of garbage. A mangy dog, skin stretched tautly over its ribs, sniffs for scraps of food. At the far side of the road a lazy wire fence slants. Beyond the fence lies the desert, covered with a blanket of rust-colored scrub.

This is where Coral's body was discarded. The desert stretches until it reaches a gray silhouette of mountains. Clouds hug the peaks. A vast pale-blue sky covers the whole scene. Fresh migrants arrive daily to make the outer reaches of Juárez their home. This open desert is theirs for the taking, and it is clear to me why this edge of nowhere is a favorite dumping ground for the murderers.

The colored newspaper dots of Coral's photograph reappear before me.

I wonder where God is in this wasteland.

The desert wind blows hot.

FOUR DISCOURSES

Four popular conceptions surround the Juarensen female workers and their murders, each giving rise to a discourse. The names of two of these discourses—the *maquiloca discourse* and the *maquiladora discourse*—are similar, but each presents a unique false belief about the victims. Added to the *maquiloca* and *maquiladora* discourses are the *backlash discourse*, which purports that these women have violated traditional gender roles causing men to lash out at them with violence, and the *culture of violence discourse*, which understands feminicides and everyday violence as interrelated and all but accepted in Mexican culture.

The **Maquiloca** *Discourse*

Maquiloca is a colloquialism in Juárez that combines two Spanish terms: *maquiladora* (assembly plant) and *loca* (crazy). The *maquiloca* discourse asserts that female *maquiladora* workers "go crazy," embarking on a so-called wild life now obtainable due to their increased income. By implying that the victims are at least somewhat to blame for their own misfortune, this slanderous epithet for female *maquiladora* workers has hindered public discourse on the feminicides.

Most of the thousands of female *maquiladora* laborers in Juárez are rural migrants to the border metropolis. Their recently attained status as workers, with both its benefits and associated responsibilities, is a shift from the traditional roles of Mexican women. Externally, these women now have an income, along with workplace peers. Internally, they have begun to forge new identities and have obtained the power to challenge certain cultural conventions, such as living under the supervision of parents, a husband, or a boyfriend. Joining the labor force garners for them a newfound liberty.

The *maquiloca* discourse distorts these facts. For example, part of the discourse is the inaccurate assumption that the *maquiloca*'s wages are sufficient to make her self-supporting; if not a household breadwinner, she is earning enough to support a husband or boyfriend. But the truth is that these women are paid only US$4 to $5 per day, a sum inadequate for even one person to live a safe and healthy life.[2]

But the chief focus of the *maquiloca* discourse concerns the *maquiloca*'s supposed over-involvement in Juárez nightlife. Sociologist Linda Rosa Fregoso attests that Mexican women going out to clubs and bars is nothing new,[3] but the *maquiloca* discourse claims that women are using their newly gained salaries to finance a "party" lifestyle in which they may use their newfound liberty in a manner that leads them down an adventurous but ultimately destructive path of self-discovery. Juárez's bars and clubs are depicted as fertile ground for such experimentation. In the metroplex these women are (so the discourse goes) further exposed to American cultural values—something that traditional

Mexican opinion holds to be a significant contributor to Mexico's purported moral decline.[4]

By this logic, impressionable young women undergo a transformation from rural migrants to wayward party girls consorting with shady border lowlifes as they dance the night away. They are carrying on a double life: by day the *maquiloca* is a "dutiful daughter, wife, mother, sister, and laborer, but by night she reveals her inner prostitute, slut, and barmaid."[5] Thus the women tempt death by inviting it to their doorstep.

The *maquiloca* discourse's exaggerated portrayal of the freedom enjoyed by the working woman of Juárez overlooks the limits and responsibilities of her life. It does not take into account the challenges she faces to balance the responsibilities of workplace and home. For example, a worker in a *maquiladora* averages a forty-five-hour work week, not counting the lengthy commutes that are almost invariably involved in getting to and from the factories. As for participation in Juárez nightlife, night shifts are the norm for the *maquiladora* worker; Juárez teems with nighttime commuters traveling hazardous streets and bus routes.[6]

The *maquiloca* discourse is commonly heard in the Juarensen community and also regularly employed by politicians, official investigators, and religious leaders to exonerate the failures of Mexico's infrastructure, as well as to explain the alleged moral decline in Juárez. This rhetorical strategy shifts attention away from the systemic corruption and overall failures of Mexican government and society, replacing those failures with the idea of the victims being "fallen women." As Melissa W. Wright, professor of geography and women's studies at Pennsylvania State University, puts it: "When one finds girls and women out on the streets at night, seeking adventure, dancing in clubs and free from parental vigilance, one finds evidence of diminished value in their wasted innocence, their wasted loyalty, and their wasted virginity."[7]

Wright notes that the *maquiloca* discourse recreates "the possibility that these women and girls are not only victims of a culture out of whack but are also emblems of the loss of values." This is tied to another of the discourse's damaging declarations: that the *maquilocas* "represent culture value in decline and therefore may not be valuable enough in death to warrant much concern." In short, the victim is not worthy of worry. And since she is of so little worth, what need is there to pursue her killer? Such a course of action might restore the cultural values whose erosion these women represent.[8]

The Maquiladora *Discourse*

The *maquiladora* discourse describes a female Mexican factory worker who fluctuates between value and waste in the labor force, but whose eventual fate is to be used up by the *maquiladora* industry and then discarded.[9] This discourse does not offer a direct explanation of the feminicides but focuses on how the *maquiladora* industry exploits females by offering them a "no win" scenario. This discourse also frames the Mexican working woman, once again, as not worthy of worry—in the workplace or as a murder victim—because she represents waste.

Approximately 60 percent of *maquiladora* employees are women.[10] Operating on the (mistaken) premise that all of the murder victims are *maquiladora* workers, the *maquiladora* discourse frames the phenomenon with a mercenary logic,[11] labeling Mexican women as some of the most sought-after laborers in Latin America, with their nimble fingers, the attention to detail that they are able to devote for the duration of lengthy shifts, their eagerness for work, and their docility and submissiveness to the patriarchy of their work environment.

According to the *maquiladora* discourse, the downside of having a female component in the workforce is that women workers are intrinsically flawed: they are "nervous," they lack the ambition necessary for promotion to management, and worst of all, they are "untrainable." This last claim pertains less to specific occupational skills than to the perception that women cannot cultivate the company loyalty that would make them worthy of long-term positions.[12]

Whether deserved or not, the fact that large numbers of female *maquiladora* workers move from company to company has contributed to this perception of disloyalty and a subsequent decline in women's worth as employees. Mexican women have come to represent a permanent labor force of the temporarily employed. To use Wright's phrase, female factory workers in Mexico face a "debilitating journey of labor turnover."[13]

By comparison, the value of the male worker appreciates over time. He is perceived as an ambitious, trainable, and loyal employee "who will support the high-tech transformation of the maquila sector throughout the twenty-first century. He maintains his value as he changes and develops in a variety of ways."[14] And so he naturally advances up the occupational ladder.

Wright argues that women laborers are "pigeonholed" by the *maquiladora* industry's focus on them as "intrinsically untrainable." She notes that these women earn the lowest wages and have the most dead-end jobs. Wright suggests introducing concrete changes into the work environment that would curb these stereotypes and address women's labor-related interests, such as competitive wages, training programs, daycare centers, flexible work schedules, attention to repetitive-stress disorder, and establishing a humane maternity policy.[15]

Maternity leaves are a flashpoint in the workplace. *Maquiladora* administrators monitor women's reproductive cycles by having them undergo a pregnancy test during the application process and monthly tests once they are employed. Reports Wright, "Although illegal, harassment of pregnant women is common, which demonstrates that noticeably pregnant women are ripe for turnover."[16] Although for over three decades the Mexican *maquiladora* industry has depended on the mass of temporary female workers, these women have nonetheless remained victims of industrial exploitation. Wright sums up their dilemma: "Mexican women thus represent workers of declining value since their intrinsic value never appreciates into skills but instead dissipates over time. Their value is used up, not enhanced. Consequently, the Mexican woman personifies waste in the making, as the materials of her body gain shape through the discourses that explain how she is untrainable, unskillable and always a temporary worker."[17]

Journalist Debbie Nathan notes that within *maquiladoras,* sexual harassment, provocative dress, and flirtatious behavior between male supervisors and female subordinates are commonplace, with women even competing for male supervisors' attention. This milieu perpetuates what Nathan labels "rigid femininity." By way of example, she offers the industry-wide *Señorita Maquiladora* beauty contest, complete with gown and swimsuit competitions.[18]

Wright draws a compelling parallel between the treatment of women in the industrial cycle and the feminicides themselves. In both cases the Mexican woman becomes a figure that can be disposed of once her value has been extracted. As inherently a "figure of waste," she exculpates the *maquiladora* industry from responsibility for her exploitation.[19]

We can observe an extension of such a perspective in the industry's failure to take measures to stop the killings. For example, many victims of the feminicides were abducted while commuting to or from work, yet the *maquiladora* industry has made no effort to improve women's safety. It seems that Mexican working women are not sufficiently valued to be saved from serial killings, since when a woman leaves or is lost a multitude of temporary workers is waiting to replace her.

The Backlash Discourse

Unlike the two first two discourses, the backlash discourse is valid—although it is surely not recognized as such in Mexico.

In the context of my argument, "backlash" refers to the retaliatory rage that some men vent on women in an attempt to compensate for their own sense of "failed masculinity."[20] In the backlash discourse, women have violated traditional gender roles in both the workplace and the home; men, in response to the collapse of their patriarchal constructs and control over women, retaliate violently. Since a man's backlash is generally aimed at his romantic partner, the hundreds of women killed in Juárez in acts of targeted sexual violence suggest a pathology of male aggressiveness that is maniacal.

Machismo refers to domineering male attitudes that evince themselves in exaggerated and often contradictory behaviors. This familiar term occasions a variety of both popular and scholarly interpretations.[21] In the early 1970s Evelyn P. Stevens broke ground by coining the term *marianismo*, a female companion to *machismo*.[22] *Marianismo* indicates Latina behavior patterns of submission and self-abnegation. Stevens maintains that *marianismo* "is just as prevalent as machismo but less understood by Latin Americans themselves and almost unknown to foreigners. This cult of feminine spiritual superiority teaches that women are semi-divine, and morally superior to and spiritually stronger than men."[23] Part of the interrelated phenomena of *machismo* and *marianismo* is the "dynamic interplay" between male dominance and female submissiveness, with both genders asserting superiority by way of this dynamic. The male controls with his psychic and physical strength, while the female claims a spiritual and moral advantage by being submissive and self-abnegating.[24]

In recent years gender dynamics have undergone an unprecedented shift in Mexico—a shift linked to increasing industrialization. This is particularly true in Juárez, where the North American Free Trade Agreement (NAFTA) triggered an economic boom that altered the labor force dramatically. One major change was that thousands of men lost their jobs to women.

Like women, men in Juárez must contend with rampant poverty, poor living conditions, and long and dangerous commutes. This combination of factors has resulted in a vastly demoralized local male population that feels powerless to vent its rage on the nebulous global economic regime. Some of these demoralized males instead find the nearest vulnerable target: a woman.[25]

Of course, the closest woman is often in the man's own home. In post-NAFTA Mexico, women's new roles and responsibilities test conventional gender identities, a scenario that generates domestic tension. According to Staudt, "Women who continue working after getting married challenge the once-sacred household division of labor because they cannot tend husbands and children in once-idealized ways."[26]

A new kind of Mexican woman has emerged in Ciudad Juárez. Work, money, and new relationships (so the discourse goes) offer her an identity and liberty that previous generations would not have imagined. This makes her far less likely to accept the naturalized ideology of female subservience. And although her wages are meager and she often works out of need rather than choice, she nonetheless earns and controls money, which gives her increased leverage within the new gender dynamics.[27] The result is that these women—typically very young—may threaten or even unseat men as household breadwinners.[28] Mexican men accustomed to a dominant role over women now confront the practical and psychological collapse of their time-honored traditions and identities. Hence the backlash.

Staudt understands this backlash as "a desperate and flawed strategy to regain power."[29] As is the case worldwide, the majority of women murdered in Juárez are victims of domestic violence.[30] But the backlash discourse also attempts to explain feminicides that are not the direct result of domestic violence, appealing to evidence that the victims' bodies show more than simple murders, transgressing to exaggerated and even maniacal behavior. Often the corpses are mutilated, burned, and discarded near city intersections. Journalist Charles Bowden contributes to the backlash discourse with his customary edginess: "Killing girls has, in effect, become what men of Juárez do with the frustrations of living in a town with . . . abundant poverty. It is the local language of rage, a blood price exacted for what Juárez is: the world's largest border community, with 300 maquila plants, and the highest concentration of maquila workers in the country."[31]

The Culture of Violence Discourse

The culture of violence discourse reaffirms that we should understand feminicides and everyday violence as interrelated.[32] It focuses on the effect this violence has on the local community, engendering an environment deadly to women. The discourse acknowledges various factors that impose structural and physical violence on the people of Juárez, and that these factors are so prevalent that civic life has assimilated violence to the point of making it a normative and acceptable course of action for the average citizen. In such a culture woman-killing is permissible.

Worse, the average citizen accepts violence as a matter of course. For example, domestic violence occurs with such frequency that it is rarely reported to police, much less investigated. In this culture, then, killing women is simply a matter of degree; violence against women is implicitly allowed.

More broadly, systemic violence in Juárez tacitly gives average people "permission" to engage in less egregious acts of civil misconduct, which are routinely committed without legal consequences. How inconsequential is bribing a policeman to get out of a ticket for running a red light compared to the murderous behavior of narcotraffickers? As anthropologist Howard Campbell argues, using evidence from popular culture, participation in the narco-trade—even if only partial or part-time—is routine for thousands of "average" people on both sides of the border.[33] Campbell reports:

For the border populations, drug trafficking is a tacitly tolerated activity or a mundane, everyday phenomenon that, though not fully accepted, is not considered a radically deviant or unusual lifestyle. Drug traffickers are students in high school and college, manual laborers, grandparents, shoppers and clerks in stores, waiters, teachers, and government employees. They are our neighbors, sons, mothers, cousins, friends and co-workers. They are everywhere.[34]

CONCLUSION

There are two frequently asked questions regarding the feminicides: Who is killing the women? and Why are the women being killed? Although not directly formulated as immediate responses to these questions, collectively, these discourses mute such elementary inquiries by articulating the interplay of a male-dominated society and female objectification. The discourses form a larger and dominant "patriarchal discourse."

The *maquiloca* and *maquiladora* discourses present negative and misconstrued perceptions of women that dominate the Juarensen culture. These discourses also articulate a process by which a derogatory moral judgment is cast on women's character. A woman's lesser worth allows for dismissal of her peril, going so far as to place the blame for it squarely on her shoulders. This exonerates the global economy, along with the local system of government and law enforcement that has failed to act to stop this murder spree—all while sanctifying the status quo moral standards of Mexico, whose decline these women have come to represent. The backlash discourse offers evidence that violence and often death are the result of such patriarchy and misogyny. Add in the consequences of an escalating culture of violence, and the odds for a woman from a rural community to survive in the metroplex become low. All four discourses characterize work and home environments wherein women are violated by means of objectification, devalued worth, and sexualization. They also present the fundamental reality that woman hold little more than utilitarian worth in Juárez.

These discourses also point out that the parties responsible for these deaths cannot be limited to the immediate perpetrators. The *maquiladora* industry, investors, and governmental interests must be held liable for failing to confront—and worse, arguably advancing—derogatory attitudes toward women. Such ingrained attitudes and practices demand radical changes, beginning with practical programs to inform and protect women in the workplace, during their commutes, and in their homes.

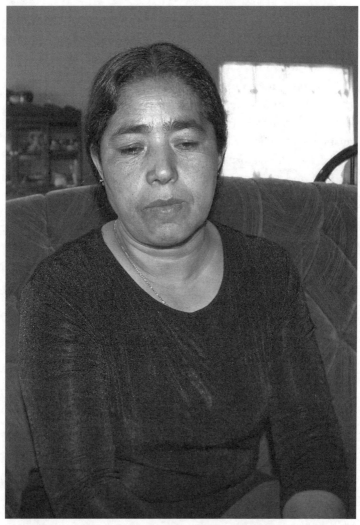

A saddened face. *Paula Bonilla-Flores's daughter Sagrario was murdered on April 10, 1998, at age seventeen. Her case has not been completely resolved, and most likely it never will be. More than 90 percent of the crimes perpetrated in Mexico in the last ten years remain unresolved.*

3

What Is Suffering?

This is the hour of lead
Remembered if outlived,
As freezing persons recollect the snow—
First chill, then stupor, then the letting go.

—EMILY DICKINSON,
"AFTER A GREAT PAIN A FORMAL FEELING COMES"

INVITATION TO A HOUSE OF DEATH,
MARCH 12, 2005

I have been invited to a house of death. It is a concrete home located in a neighborhood known as Zacatecas in the eastern outskirts of Ciudad Juárez. It's a dusty, bumpy trip on a dirt road.

At the door Paula Bonilla-Flores and Jesús González-Flores warmly welcome me into their home. The cement floor and flat, tin ceiling of the one-room house make this nothing more than a box, save for the lively Mexican-pink walls. A tiny kitchen is positioned in one corner; a dresser in the middle of the room acts as a divide for the bedroom. Paula and Jesús take what seem to be their usual places on a small, red loveseat, gently signaling me to sit across from them in a small chair. Guillermina, one of their five daughters, sits on the bed on the other side of the room, head down, fingers darting and pulling at some needle-work. Guillermina never speaks, but she hears all. Next to her is a small boy, perhaps two years old, who naps peacefully on the bed. Back across the room, their parents' hands twist and fidget.

To be invited to visit a mourning family is a privilege. In this condition people are often willing to share their deepest heartache with a stranger. Mourning is one of the most human of experiences and always seeks relief through another's comprehension. I thank Paula and Jesús for their graciousness. Neither move. I express my deepest sympathy, but the words remain suspended in utter stillness.

Every priest enters a house plagued by a tragic death holding fast to belief in the resurrection.

The González-Flores family migrated from Durango in 1995 in search of work. Sagrario, one of seven siblings (six of them female), was murdered eighteen months later. At the time she was seventeen. *Sagrario.* I cannot keep from thinking of the unfortunate irony of her name, which means "sacred receptacle." Sacredness in life, desecration in death.

Several family members, including Sagrario, were hired to work at the General Electric plant in the Bermudez Industrial Park across the city from their home. For safety's sake, they made the commute together until Sagrario, without explanation, was given a different shift.

Paula lifts her head. When our eyes meet, I speak: *"Por favor, dime que pasó el día que Sagrario se desapareció."* "Please, tell me what happened the day Sagrario disappeared."

April 10, 1998, was a Friday, and Sagrario finished work at 3:45 p.m. It is presumed that she started her trip home, a fifteen-mile commute that involved taking two eastbound buses though Ciudad Juárez and into the slum districts on the city's outer edges. Sagrario, a faithful and dutiful daughter, was always punctual. And so, when she was fifteen minutes late arriving home, Paula became panic stricken.

Paula showed me several photographs of Sagrario, an attractive young woman with shoulder-length brown hair, fine features, and a lovely smile. She fit the profile of hundreds of young women who have been targets of sexual violence in Juárez.

Paula recalls Sagrario as "very reserved. She did not have a wide circle of friends." Sagrario desired "to make more of herself," learning to play the guitar and working with computers. She volunteered at the local church, Our Lady of Guadalupe, teaching catechism to young children. "She was very kind and friendly with everyone," Paula says, including with Andrés, who worked with Sagrario in the *maquiladora* and was her first boyfriend. Paula had urged her daughter to leave the *maquiladora*, but Sagrario wanted to help support the family.

The Mexico–U.S. border is not only a port of entry for illegal drugs but also for people—many of whom are smuggled into the United States against their will. Paula feared that her daughter might have been kidnapped by sex traffickers and sold into prostitution. She spent the days immediately following Sagrario's disappearance at the border checkpoint handing out fliers to anybody who would take them. With the help of friends, family, church, and community groups, four thousand fliers were distributed.

On the second day after Sagrario's disappearance, her father and brother went to Andrés's home to see if he had seen Sagrario. Andrés assisted them in searching for her and was never a suspect in the case.

On or around April 20, José Luis Hernandez-Flores (no relation) communicated to the family that they would find Sagrario in Loma Blanca, across the city in Valle de Juárez, implying that she was already dead. Paula and Jesús knew that José Luis had asked Sagrario to be his girlfriend and that she had refused him, and so now they feared the worst. On April 29, police found Sagrario's body in a vacant lot where José Luis had said they would. She had been stabbed numerous times and strangled.

The family provided all the information it had to local police. But it was not until seven years later that police finally arrested José Luis.

Paula and Jesús believe that the motive for Sagrario's murder was her refusal of José Luis. At the time of my 2005 interview with the couple, José Luis was in custody. He had implicated three other men in Sagrario's murder, but no action had been taken against them. Sagrario's parents contend that others must have been involved in her murder; a vehicle was used in the kidnapping and transportation of Sagrario's body, and José Luis neither owned a car nor knew how to drive.[1] They believe police have not arrested José Luis's accomplices because they are *contrabandistas* (drug dealers).

News accounts and personal experience have taught Juarenses how drug smuggling works. "These men move people and drugs across the border," Jesús says. "Police are getting money from these persons, so they cannot get them for the killings." "[The police] do *know* who killed Sagrario, but they don't *want* to act," avers Paula, speculating that Sagrario's case is not an isolated instance of violence but related to all of the feminicides. "The persons who are doing this know exactly what they are doing. They have lots of practice. And they no longer have a conscience."

Paula explains that her family now lives in fear. Only reluctantly does she allow her remaining daughters to continue their education; she now accompanies them to and from school. "They no longer have a normal life," she laments. "I will only let them go out with me." Paula likens her daughters to captives but says she cannot grant them their former freedom for fear of their coming to the same end as Sagrario. "It will never be the same," she says. The daughters have even stopped practicing guitar. "They have rejected everything."

Sagrario's murder forced the family to reevaluate its relationship with God. Paula wonders, for example, how Sagrario could be kidnapped and murdered while wearing the medal of Our

Lady of Guadalupe, as she always did. Paula always assumed that the medal would keep her daughter under divine protection. "Where was God when Sagrario needed him?" she asks.

Despite her questions, Paula remains a Roman Catholic. "The only faith that I have left is in God," she says. "He is going to help us." However, although the family still goes to mass occasionally, it has largely left the church community. "I do not want to live my faith like a regimen, an obligation," Paula says.

Friends have told Paula that she must forgive the murderers because God will forgive them, but the idea disheartens her. "In the prayer, the 'Our Father,' it says to forgive," she says. "I do not pray that part, because I am not doing it. . . . Here in the world there is no justice. But I do believe in justice. In heaven there is justice." She finds some consolation in the fact that José Luis was finally arrested, but she is not satisfied. "One criminal was caught; the others [must] be, too. There is no perfect crime. There has to be justice. There has to be."

Paula has made her quest for justice a public cause. She does interviews with the news media about her ongoing investigation of Sagrario's death and her participation in the painting of pink crosses. But in rural Mexico drawing such attention to oneself—especially for women—is considered bad form. Some community members say Paula and the other victims' mothers "*hicieron mucho escandalo*" (have caused a scandal) and ought to bear their anguish with a dignified silence.

Paula's answer: "This is the only way we have to seek justice."

THREE FORMS OF SUFFERING

The English verb "to suffer" derives from the Latin *suffer_re*, which comes from the suffix *suf*, "sub," and root *ferre*, "to bear." Thus, in its most elementary signification, "to suffer" means "to bear under." The ancient Greek word for suffering, *pathai*, means "to feel," in the sense of emotions (as opposed to touch).

The English word *pathos* shares the same root and signifies "the stirring of tender or melancholy emotion."[2]

There are three types of suffering: ontological, historically imposed, and moral.[3] Each form of suffering can be either meaningful or meaningless. The suffering is meaningful if we learn something from it; the suffering is meaningless if we learn nothing.

Ontological suffering—the suffering of sickness, old age, and death[4]—is often called natural suffering. It is neither just nor unjust but simply part of human reality. From ontological suffering we learn the limits of our mortal existence. This suffering instructs us to love people with a cognizance of the limits of mortal existence. Love will always result in pain because some sort of separation—for example, betrayal or death—is inevitable. We learn what it means to love within the conditions of our existence, and in this way we learn to love well.

Historically imposed suffering demonstrates our inhumanity to one another. It is the unnecessary and unjust suffering that we see everywhere, from the war in Afghanistan to gang violence in East Los Angeles. It is also this scourge of human cruelty in Juárez, where industrialization and the drug war result in slain and missing women. Sagrario's murder and the resulting suffering of the González-Flores family are specific examples of historically imposed suffering. From observing historically imposed suffering we learn what must be done to make the world and human life more humane. Through it we learn our role in life and that each person is called to a different task.

Moral suffering describes the suffering of those who oppose historically imposed suffering. From moral suffering we learn our capabilities and that we can be agents to stop suffering. We also learn that our opposition to historically imposed suffering comes at a cost. Moral suffering is that cost. This is exemplified in Christianity by Jesus' suffering and death on the cross. Modern examples of moral suffering include that of Gandhi, Martin Luther

King, Jr., and Cesar Chavez. The contributions these figures have made to humanity teach us what we are capable of. This is a necessary lesson, because most of us would say that we are not capable of the types of action undertaken by these radical social reformers. But the real reason for our resistance and failure to act is our unwillingness to pay the cost of opposing historically imposed suffering. Once we understand that we *are* capable and accept that there will be consequences, perhaps severe ones, to opposing unjust suffering, then we can see that we can indeed be agents of change.

Ontological suffering we have to learn to accept. But we do not need to accept historically imposed suffering. Moral suffering we accept and should not flee from, because moral suffering is the path of human flourishing.

AFFLICTION

To help us further understand the experience of human suffering, I turn to French philosopher Simone Weil. Born in 1909 to an affluent and cultured family, as a youth Weil abandoned her life of privilege for solidarity with the working class. Her brilliance, ascetic life, introversion, and eccentricities limited her ability to bond with others but did not hinder her from teaching and participating in the radical political movement of her time. Her writings, particularly on suffering, were drawn from her own willingness to take on suffering.

Within the realm of human suffering Weil distinguishes a singular experience that she calls *malheur*. *Malheur* is often translated "misfortune" or "adversity," but Weil uses the word for her own purposes in discussing a concept closer to what English speakers call *affliction*, and so that is the translation we will use here. This inexactitude is not simply a linguistic matter, since Weil says that the lived experience of affliction is indescribable. And so analogy assists where synonymity fails. Weil describes affliction as "a metallic coldness" that "freezes all those it touches right to the depths of their souls." Those who experience affliction "will never find warmth again."[5]

As with most suffering, affliction is multifaceted. Weil speaks of anguish as existing in three dimensions—the physical, the psychological, and the social—each of which plays a unique role in an authentic experience of affliction, an experience that encompasses the whole person. For Weil, affliction is a definitive experience of human suffering, and the totality of these three dimensions elevates genuine affliction to the realm of spiritual experience.

The experience of Paula Bonilla-Flores surpasses mere suffering: she is permanently wounded. Suffering has seized Paula's life, uprooting her physical, psychological, and social well-being. Paula is afflicted. And although she made efforts to remain poised during our interview, I witnessed the first form of affliction in the physical manifestations of suffering overtake her during two key moments. One came while Paula recounted her daughter's death. Her severe physical discomfort was apparent from the wrenching of her hands, the wiping of her brow. Her body trembled and her voice quivered until distress finally stole her breath away and she needed a break from our conversation. She displayed similar symptoms when she shared her worry over the safety of her five living daughters. A kind of hysteria overtook her then, her voice rising in volume and pitch, with fear gripping and shaking her body.

Paula's grief has taken the form of a fight for "justice," and so her injurious experience of secular injustice has led to internal crisis; thus, she endures the second form of affliction, suffering psychologically every waking moment. Her understanding of divine justice has been stretched to the breaking point. Even the suggestion that God, in a final act of divine benevolence, will forgive her daughter's murderers disheartens Paula. (She is perhaps too unassuming to voice what would be understandable outrage.)

Her faith remains, but she suffers confusion regarding God's ways in this life. She maintains that there must somehow be a penalty for her daughter's murderers. She desperately wants to understand how evildoers can seemingly triumph in this world, with Sagrario dead and her loved ones suffering. The family thus joins the chorus of the anguished, who cling to their religious faith and who feel compelled to formulate the theodical question: What kind of almighty and good God could allow such a catastrophe?

The third dimension of affliction, according to Weil, is social degradation characterized by isolation.[6] It is uncomfortable and displeasing to be in the presence of the afflicted, and so they are often ignored, persecuted, and rejected by their friends, communities, and even relatives.

For a period of time after Saragrio's murder, family members extricated themselves from social engagements with both their parish community and the small *colonia* where they reside. They did so because instead of receiving support, the family members—especially Paula—were criticized and ostracized. Paula's inability to forgive her daughter's murderers is contrary to the Christian law of love, and thus at odds with the family's Catholic parish community. The parish members believe that the family should move from pain to forgiveness.

There are many possible reasons for the community's behavior, but Weil explains that those who have not experienced anguish find it incomprehensible and are therefore unable to offer compassion to those who do. Understandably, the community's critical reaction to the family's anguish antagonizes them. In a small community of rural migrants, community members view Paula's participation in civil protests and media interviews—including a documentary—as defying the social norm of their humble lives. Paula's activities are judged excessive, pretentious, and egoistical, and the family is shunned for expressing its anguish. Weil's remark that "if a hen is hurt, the others rush upon it, attacking it with their beaks" is apposite.[7]

Another factor differentiates affliction from other human suffering and contributes to its spiritual nature: affliction is the torment of those powerless to ameliorate their own suffering. For those who have done nothing to incur that suffering, the affliction is magnified, because the suffering itself, the cause of which is beyond them, is further proof of their powerlessness. Job bore affliction when tested by God; Jesus knew affliction in Gethsemane the night before he died.

Weil insists that affliction is not genuine if it does not "take possession of the soul and mark it through and through with its own particular mark."[8] A pain that leaves no trace is a pain that was never there. Common examples of this are toothaches and gall stones; once the pain passes, so does its memory and effect upon the person.[9] Jacob wrestled throughout the night with an angel, and though he lived to witness the dawn, he was left forever wounded. Weil points out that even the resurrected body of Jesus bore the gashes of his passion.[10] Thus does Weil liken the severity of true affliction to death itself: "Affliction is an uprooting of life, a more or less attenuated equivalent of death, made irresistibly present to the soul by the attack or immediate apprehension of physical pain."[11]

After Sagrario's death, Paula believes that she and her family will never be same. Her understanding of and relationship with God are irreversibly altered. Although her wound may eventually heal, she can never return to where she was while Sagrario lived. She must bear the scar of her daughter's murder for the rest of her life.

INNOCENCE

For Weil, innocence is integral to true affliction. While suffering of any caliber compels us to ponder the nature of existence, the affliction of the innocent sharpens the theodical questions. The retributional suffering of the evildoer is understandable, but the cries of the innocent are quite another matter. Torment of the innocent upsets our assumptions about the actions of an all-powerful God; the cries of the innocent undo our presumed notions of God's benevolence. Those who suffer affliction beckon from a place of "metallic coldness" to an apparently absent God.

In the theological tradition of suffering, the biblical story of Job offers a paradigm of the innocent in torment. Job is a good man, and yet every manner of malady and woe befalls him. Job is approached, counseled, and eventually taunted by seeming friends who can only rightly be called "worthless theologians" and "sorry comforters."[12] These counselors judge Job to be guilty of terrible sin and maintain that his suffering is God's unmistakable retribution for his sin. Their judgment is based on the theological presuppositions of a God who acts only in terms of reward and punishment. They remain blind to human testimony of the experience of this upright man before them. Throughout his ordeal Job never wavers from the conviction of his innocence; nor does adversity cause Job to lose his innocence. Job's innocence is founded on his personal integrity.

The innocence of the victims of the Juárez-Chihuahua feminicides is not based on the women's individual moral integrity; it is grounded in their victimhood, which is a combination of complex factors beyond their control. Specific features distinguish their innocence. More than anything else, it is gender that determined their fate. In life, they were trodden by patriarchal societal norms, and they died at the hands of men. In the cases of targeted sexual violence, the victims were typically young—often mere girls—and defenseless. These cases are noted for the sadistic torture that occurred prior to the killings, the brutality of the killings themselves, and the subsequent desecration of the women's bodies.

Since 1993 these individual tragedies have played out hundreds of times. Sagrario is a case in point, a victim of targeted sexual violence, poverty, marginalization, and gender discrimination at the hands not only of her immediate killers but also of an entire system that created a deadly environment for her community—particularly its women.

Clarification of the women's innocence is important for several reasons. Suffering confounds human beings. Pain can unfurl in a dubious internal logic. The first line of questioning ponders why this suffering has been inflicted: Why me? or Why these innocent women? The sufferer begins to examine his or her moral state based on the rationale that suffering comes as retribution from God: What did I do to deserve this? This is an instinctive human response. But to imply that the Juárez-Chihuahua feminicides are in any way an act of divine retribution implicates God as inflicting suffering on the innocent.

ALIENATION

German theologian Dorothee Soelle was fifteen when World War II ended. Although she never participated in any Third Reich activities, when the extent of Nazi crimes was finally revealed to the world, she could only voice her "ineradicable shame." The "hollow answer" of her generation in response to this suffering moved Soelle to dedicate her life to addressing this searing theological question.[13] Soelle's *Suffering* has become one of the leading post-Shoah theologies on suffering.

In her theology Soelle adopts Weil's notion of affliction. Soelle also draws upon the work of sociologist Melvin Seeman, whose study of alienation has become a sociological standard.[14]

Soelle's theology operates out of the fundamental conviction that unnecessary suffering must be eliminated. She employs Seeman's work to critique certain social presuppositions and roles—for example, the faithful wife in an abusive marriage—that she believes can impose unnecessary suffering, but she offers no practical means of eliminating it.

Soelle explores alienation from a perspective Seeman calls "social role theory," which he describes as a narrowing of one's identity to conform to a social role due to exterior social pressure. In such a scenario, a person suffers an entrapment by a social role from which seemingly there is no escape.[15] For example, in Paula's traditional Mexican community, her presumed role as mother of a victim is that of a silent and subservient sufferer. This societal imposition and the acceptance by the individual of such a role results in a suffering that can be classified as *alienation*.

According to Soelle, alienation takes two variant forms: *powerlessness* and *meaninglessness*.[16] Consciousness of one's own powerlessness is fundamental to this classification, and such consciousness serves to increase the suffering in question.[17] To relieve this powerlessness, the person must be enabled to take action, even—perhaps especially—when faced with overwhelming circumstances, such as the *maquiladora* industry or Juárez's rampant street violence. Paula has demonstrated consciousness of the entrapment she faces in her community.

The social role Paula is supposed to enact would limit her from expressing her present inability to forgive Sagrario's murders and even from allowing herself such a conscious reaction. Such role fulfilling would also prevent her from rupturing this powerlessness by way of her protesting and pressing the Mexican police to take action. After Sagrario's death, survival for Paula meant abandoning the social role of a subservient Mexican woman. But although Paula has escaped the alienation that Seeman and Soelle address, she now faces another form of the same malady: rejection by her community.

Meaninglessness as a further dimension of alienation occurs when an individual no longer knows what to believe. Juárez is a volatile and violent place. In an unstable environment the González-Flores family members are unable to predict the outcome of acting on fundamental presuppositions because they do not know their fate from one day to the next. For Paula, this meaninglessness extends beyond her sociological reality to her theological understanding of God. Her confounded beliefs leave her without a dependable system for decision making, and so she suffers the plight of meaninglessness.

Soelle ponders "whether role theory is capable of providing sufficient insight into such suffering." Yet she also astutely observes that suffering inflicted by a society is generally perceived as one's destiny—for example, as a dutiful wife in an abusive marriage.[18] The challenge is to forge some means of liberation from these societal roles. But this is no simple task.

The backlash discourse described in the previous chapter shows that merely moving from one social role to another does not necessarily resolve this suffering. Changes in societal attitudes and individual roles come with a price, as in the case of the thousands of women in Juárez who attempt to balance the roles of laborer, wife/girlfriend, and mother. Thus, alienation requires another level of responses, which will be explored later in this work.[19]

CONCLUSION

In 2005, Sagrario's family encouraged Chihuahua state police to arrest a suspect in the crime, José Luis Hernandez, who was sentenced to 28 years in prison for the young woman's murder last year. But [Paula] Bonilla Flores, who said she was only notified of the sentence after making a special trip to the state prosecutor's office, quickly added that several other suspects in Sagrario's slaying were still free.

In May 2007, prompted by the numerous irregularities in the murder investigation of her daughter, Bonilla Flores filed a complaint against the Mexican government with the Washington, D.C.–based Inter-American Commission on Human Rights, the official human rights agency of the Organization of American States. Closer to home, Bonilla Flores and other relatives of femicide victims recently painted emblematic pink-background crosses along Ciudad Juarez's new Camino Real highway and, inspired by the Argentine mothers of the disappeared, began holding regular protests on the first Thursday of every month outside the offices of the Office of the Chihuahua State Attorney.[20]

PART II

THE CALL

Part I considered the Juárez-Chihuahua feminicides partly through the use of interpretive discourses on globalization, morals, and values, bringing into focus the complex web of circumstances and causes surrounding the killings. Framed as a theological event, the feminicides challenge us to consider what God is disclosing through this reign of terror. This revelation issues a twofold call. First, we must search for a comprehensive and humane theology of suffering to make sense out of the suffering and the killings of hundreds of women. Second, we must take the actions necessary to stop the killings.

Part II surveys various theological responses to human suffering, specifically as they relate to the feminicides. Most often these theologies of suffering are derived from one or more representations of God, representations that cover a vast theological range. For example, God understood as the just Judge—a representation that has endured throughout the ages—is one of the primary sources of the doctrine of retribution, an understanding of God as One who punishes sin with suffering.

Theism continues to struggle to reconcile the understandings of God as both all powerful and all benevolent. As we shall see, some theologians view the vindication of God's ways and not the alleviation of human suffering as the goal of these theologies. This book attempts to make theological and practical sense out of the affliction of these missing and dead women. I seek to understand what God is revealing in the catastrophe occurring in Northern

Mexico, searching for a theology of suffering that offers a credible response to this horror, one that provides the surviving victims—which, in the end, includes all members of the human family—with not only consolation but also aid in opposing and ending this needless suffering. Such a theology would portray God's compassion and solidarity with all sufferers. Furthermore, I look for an appropriate response to the human suffering that touches each of our lives.

Posting for hope: Julia Hernández-Hernández. *Thousands of electric poles, phone booths, and store windows throughout the city show photos of missing women.*

4

What Is God's Relationship to Suffering?

God is love.

—John 4:8

JULIA HERNÁNDEZ-HERNÁNDEZ

Cars honk as, dodging traffic, I cross a busy Juárez street. When I reach the cement divider, I snap a quick picture of a poster on the light pole. AYUDADANOS A ENCONTRADLA, the poster announces: *Help us find her.* In the middle of the poster there is a photograph of the missing young woman, beneath which I read her name and age: JULIA HERNÁNDEZ-HERNÁNDEZ: 20 AÑOS DE EDAD. A description follows. Julia's makeshift headshot is taken from a photo that has been grossly enlarged and obviously cropped to cut others out of the scene. Julia's oval-shaped face looks un-natural to me. I am not immediately sure why. Her hair is neatly parted down the middle and pulled tightly back, most likely in a ponytail; her ears are tucked inconspicuously underneath her hair. Yet as I study Julia's elliptical face, I see that her unusual appearance is not due wholly to her hairstyle. In part, she looks this way because the sun has bleached the poster, fading her features. Only the flat outline of a colorless white face is left. Her nose and lips appear as slender shadows; the curvature of her eyebrows has vanished. Julia stares at me. Her eye makeup has kept her vacant gaze intact. Dark pupils are enclosed by pale irises. Only a faint gray chin line separates the round of her face from her neck. I notice a rusty wire bent around the middle of the poster, securing it in place, the twisted ends poking out. Plastic tape also holds the poster to the pole. It seems to me that Julia's ghost is held captive in the faded poster.

Those who search for her still remember what Julia wore August 1, 2004, the day she disappeared: blue print pants, a floral-printed blouse, white tennis shoes. She was last seen at Colonia Heredia in Juárez. The poster lists various telephone numbers to call with any information regarding Julia, as well as the name of a relative who waits to hear, Señora Maria Eva Hernandez, presumably her mother. Julia has been relegated to a murky abyss of absence. She has become a *desaparecida*—a woman who has disappeared.

The untimely death or disappearance of any young woman is necessarily subject to the suspicion of foul play. The possibility—however unlikely—that Julia ran off with a boyfriend leaves a feeble bit of hope that she might still be alive. But if she was kidnapped, statistics show that her remains are unlikely to be found. The lack of information about her plight has most likely led to quick dismissal of her case. Since 1993, there have been approximately 250 to 300 cases of *desaparecidas* in the Juárez area.

I ponder Julia's absence. Where do we start when trying to make sense of the horrific suffering inflicted upon these young women and their relatives, friends, and communities? Julia and hundreds of other missing and dead women can never be replaced, yet loved ones must carry on. Collectively, these hundreds of absent women leave an abyss in humanity. We must turn neither from this abyss nor the difficult questions it poses; we must ask why. Our consideration of the issue in some way puts us in touch with these women's suffering.

Who is responsible for these missing women? The first ones accountable are, of course, the abductors. Other complex and interrelated factors of the sociopolitical and economic environment create a further toxic reality for women, and the drug cartel's violence plays a key role in escalating the danger for all Juarenses, particularly women.

Yet asking the hows and whys about these missing women ultimately raises the question of God's relationship to the suffering in Juárez—and more generally to all human suffering. Has God abandoned the borderlands while women are being kidnapped and murdered? Do the drug wars rage and the poor suffer without divine interest? Did God send this suffering as punishment for the licentiousness that goes on at the border? Are these woman-killings a punishment for sin? Maybe the purpose of these killings is to instruct Ciudad Juárez in some divine lesson à la Sodom and Gomorrah. If so, why does God allow the innocent to be singled out for such dreadful victimization?

Each of these questions and the responses to them employ various theologies that have developed in the long and rich tradition of the exploration of human suffering. This chapter considers the purported purposes of suffering inherent in the Juárez-Chihuahua feminicides by weighing this suffering against three traditional representations of God: the just Judge, the supreme Educator, and the inscrutable God. These theological rationales for suffering—commonly referred to as the three acquittals, since their aim is to justify God's relation to human suffering—are vividly dramatized in the Book of Job, and we find a specific theology of suffering derived from each.

Kristiaan Depoortere, a professor of pastoral theology at the Catholic University of Leuven, has deconstructed these three acquittals in *A Different God: A Christian View of Suffering*.[1] Depoortere considers what he refers to as the "value" and "disvalue" of each of these three perspectives. Depoortere's significant contribution to the theology of suffering is his pastoral understanding of these three acquittals as they relate to what he calls the "sense and nonsense of pain and suffering."[2]

THE JUST JUDGE

The representation of God as just Judge is an un-nuanced understanding of the Divine that focuses on a single divine attribute of God—all just, the guardian and guarantor of a system of immanent justice.[3] This presentation is the primary source of *the doctrine of retribution*, the teaching that "sin is followed by suffering."[4] God becomes a moralistic Divinity, understood as the grand Bookkeeper in a relationship with humankind. God's relationship with humankind is played out in terms of insult and appeasement, guilt and expiation, crime and punishment. This notion employs theological terms such as *retribution*, *atonement*, *expiation*, and *ransom*.[5] In times of crisis, this representation is reflected in remarks like, What did I do to deserve this? This instinctual logic assumes that "payback time" has come: the just Judge is "getting back" at the individual for his or her past sins. In this representation God wins souls by chastening them, and submission to this punishment is the appropriate response.

This understanding of the Divine has ancient roots and is most famously dramatized in the biblical narrative of Job.[6] Torment befalls the main character. When Job's friends confront him by asking the nature of his sin, Job stubbornly insists upon his innocence. In other words, Job has done nothing worthy of incurring God's wrath, nothing deserving of punishment. Job's response is interpreted as arrogance. Job's friends Eliphaz, Bildad, and Zophar respond to his plight in chapters 4 through 27 with a series of speeches wherein each interprets God's actions toward Job. Their narrow theological understanding is voiced with bold certitude; they are filled with conceit. Eliphaz speaks: "Reflect now: what innocent person perishes? Since when are the upright destroyed? As I see it, those who plow for mischief and sow trouble, reap the same. By the breath of God they perish, and by the blast of his wrath they are consumed" (Job 4:7–9).

There is understandable appeal and value in this representation of the Divine, which explains—at least in part—why it has endured and exercised such influence for ages.[7] The notion of God as just Judge seems to clarify the ineffable mystery of human suffering. There is a cause-and-effect relationship between sin and suffering. Good behavior is rewarded, while bad behavior provokes punishment. Behavior and its consequences are linked in a clear, determined order. And since no one is innocent of sin, all are subject to punishment. Thus, an acceptable explanation for suffering in the world has been offered, and all is in order.[8] Depoortere points out, "By means of this theory, those who suffer are able to exercise a certain intellectual control over uncontrollable reality, even in the midst of their despair."[9] If suffering is retribution, it is comprehensible.

But the just Judge representation requires closer examination. It presents the Divine as limited and one dimensional. The divine image is distorted by making judgment and punishment the dominant divine attributes while compromising Divine love. This God, who sets the world aright by means of punishment and reward, is stripped of any genuine mercy or compassion for humankind. Furthermore, the just Judge representation functions on the dangerous presumption that suffering always comes as a punishment for sin, and for no other reason. With such a belief system in place, the sufferer has no need to understand genuine guilt and punishment nor to desire anything other than to submit to the suffering—which, after all, is the will of God.

Additionally, this representation of God opens the door to neurotic guilt and the self-torturing attitudes that are present in some Christian spiritualities.[10] Freudian critiques of religion center on the just Judge notion. God is reduced to that "greater" earthly father, he who accuses and punishes, consoles and protects. This God, who acts in an all-too-human manner, is minimized into some sort of petty accountant.[11]

The most disturbing part of this notion is that it legitimizes the injustice of subjecting the innocent to suffering, presuming that their sinful actions are the reasons for their just affliction. Such is the case for Job, and so also those sufferers who presume their pain befalls them because they have displeased God and invoked divine wrath. Suffering is their punishment. This logic condemns sufferers to search for and struggle with the neurotic image of themselves as the cause of their own punishment. This neurosis is seemingly confirmed when they see those who are the true causes of the afflictions of the innocent not only go unpunished but also succeed in their wicked endeavors.

God considered as the just Judge makes meaningless the distinction between suffering that can be eliminated and that which cannot. Human initiative is thereby paralyzed. Resignation ensues, quelling any meaningful battle against suffering.[12] This representation is not of a loving God, and it leads the believer to adopt one of two possible stances: unhealthy submission to or rebellion against God. It is impossible to weigh the damage this notion has inflicted.

Jesus dismisses this notion of divine retribution in the narrative of the Man Born Blind in John's Gospel (9:1–41). When Jesus and his apostles come upon a man who has been blind from birth, his disciples presume that the man's malady is the consequence of sin. They question Jesus regarding the origin of this blind man's punishment: "'Rabbi, was it his sin or that of his parents that caused him to be born blind?' 'Neither,' answered Jesus: 'It was no sin either of this man or of his parents.'"

THE SUPREME EDUCATOR

The representation of God as supreme Educator takes a step forward in understanding God as a loving and not merely a punishing God. Suffering is not God's revenge but an invitation to conversion. Suffering is medicinal.[13] The aim of this suffering is to bring about a cure. It is the bitter pill that will heal sufferers and ultimately offer them a better life. Common counsels that emerge from this rationale echo in refrains such as "God tests the ones he loves" and "God never sends more suffering than we can deal with."[14]

The representation of the supreme Educator is valid and well grounded in the scriptural tradition. We can learn from suffering. The difficulty with this theological premise is the possibility of a distorted application to explain suffering.[15] The Book of Job dramatizes this theological understanding of suffering as a complex spiritual tug of war: God allows Satan to test Job. Eliphaz speaks: "Behold, happy is the man whom God reproves! The Almighty chastening do not reject. For he wounds, but he binds up; he smites, but his hands give healing" (Job 5:17–18a).

The Book of Wisdom offers this similar instruction: "For if before men, indeed, they be punished, yet is their hope full of immortality; Chastised a little, they shall be greatly blessed, because God tried them and found them worthy of himself. As gold in the furnace, he proved them" (Wis 3:4–6). And the Epistle to the Hebrews offers another corresponding instruction: "Do not disdain the discipline of the Lord nor lose heart when he reproves you; For whom the Lord love, he disciplines; he scourges every son he receives" (Heb 12:5b–6).

Here, suffering is linked to time. The reality of suffering is always rooted in present pain, but this representation looks to the future. That God as the supreme Educator justifies present pain with its future lesson or reward suggests a denial of that current suffering. Both feminist and liberation theologies have strongly criticized this understanding.[16]

This rationale can be applied to the understanding that suffering endured in this earthly "valley of tears" will be rewarded in heaven. While this may be true, most often it offers little consolation to the person in pain. The question at hand is not heaven's divine reward but rather a manner of "consolation" that can minimize the sufferer's present affliction. True compassion is a sharing of the sufferer's pain in the present moment. Furthermore, the response to suffering understood as pedagogical must again be submission, because suffering was sent by God for the good of the sufferer. Thereby, the representation of God as the supreme Educator undercuts the motivation to battle against suffering.

Depoortere observes three constructive values from this pedagogical theology of suffering:

1. Suffering strengthens the sufferer. This is the "no pain, no gain" philosophy. Trial forges character.
2. Suffering serves as an alarm. This idea suggests that bodily distress, for example, is indicative of a more serious malady. Pain announces the call for immediate action. The attentive person is awakened by pain and thus seeks healing or resolution.
3. Suffering makes people more altruistic; for example, a recovering alcoholic who converts to Christianity, a prisoner who learns a life lesson after pondering his or her crime, or the person who has a near-death experience that subsequently alters his or her lifestyle. Such genuinely moving experiences should not be undervalued. Such suffering may dramatically change a person's life.[17]

The pedagogical character of certain sufferings can indeed be richly beneficial to human experience. Often we do learn from our mistakes, and character can be forged through hardship. Consideration of suffering-as-pedagogy certainly gives meaning and purpose to pain. The problem with this logic is that it cannot be the final word on suffering.[18] Learning a meaningful lesson from one's suffering does not eradicate the inherent difficulty in accepting the idea that God sends suffering as a test. After all, there comes to pass at least an equal amount of suffering that does *not* positively change the sufferer. As Depoortere points out, "The risk of not growing at all is much greater."[19] Some may be purified by their suffering, but others are left embittered; some awaken with the alarm, while others flee; some cast off selfishness, but others become more self-involved. The negative prospect of *not* learning from suffering always lurks within the consideration of suffering as entirely meted out by a God solely for educational purposes. In and of itself, suffering guarantees neither learning nor conversion.

THE INSCRUTABLE GOD

The inscrutable God is a benevolent deity who acts in a manner that is beyond humankind's comprehension. This representation aims to acquit God of the guilt of human suffering.[20] It is based on the infinite disparity between God and humankind. Although God and humanity are in relation, we are not equal. God acknowledges the reality of human suffering but offers no explanation, since God's intentions are beyond human understanding. Within this theological representation, *mystery* is the central premise. God is incomprehensible, and as a consequence, the reason for suffering remains a mystery.

At the close of the Book of Job, in a whirlwind theophany, God finally addresses Job. This encounter is conducted with divine, not human, protocol. God addresses Job; God will not be questioned by Job. God wastes no time with small talk. God offers no account of any action taken toward Job:

> Who is this that obscures divine plans with
> words of ignorance?
> Gird up your loins now, like a man; I will ques-
> tion you, and you tell me the answer!

> Where were you when I founded the earth? Tell
>   me, if you have understanding.
> Who determined its size: do you know? Who
>   stretched out the measuring line for it?
>   . . .
> Have you ever in your lifetime commanded the
>   morning and shown the dawn its place
> For taking hold of the end of the earth, till the
>   wicked are shaken from its surface? . . .
> Have you entered into the sources of the sea, or
>   walked about in the depths of the abyss?
> Have the gates of death been shown to you,
>   or have you seen the gates of darkness?
>   (Job 38:2–5, 12–13, 16–17)

Isaiah's famous words also capture this notion of the inscrutable God:

> For my thoughts are not your thoughts,
>   nor are your ways my ways, says the Lord.
> For as the heavens are higher than the earth,
>   so are my ways higher than your ways
>   and my thoughts than your thoughts.
>   (Isa 55:8–9)

Neither punishment nor pedagogy drives the inscrutable
God, nor do facile rationales offer an account for divine ways.
Rather, this representation demonstrates a development in the
way humankind understands its divine experience, because both
the Divine and suffering itself retain the essential character of
mystery.

By not relying on the rationale of punishment or pedagogy
to explain the causes of pain, the theology of this representation respects suffering as a profound mystery. Suffering is no

longer a problem that can be easily circumscribed by a single, all-encompassing logic, nor can it be reduced to a cause-and-effect equation. Analysis and reason also come up short.[21] By respecting its mysterious nature, suffering becomes an encounter that can be engaged only as the most profound of human experiences.

This theology of suffering does not explain away or impose unfounded meaning on suffering, and so the experiencing of the pain is not trivialized.[22] The inscrutable God retains divine benevolence, to the degree that the Divine remains attached to the tears and blood of the anguishing, to their helplessness. Since suffering is neither punitive nor pedagogical, pain comes without the baggage of inflicting guilt or teaching a life lesson. No price must be paid; no God must be appeased to relieve the pain. The love of an inscrutable God does not pivot on punishment or reward. As Job loved God in spite of the trials that befell him, the sufferer is invited to journey the same path of spiritual maturity. Divinity is no longer a utilitarian God employed merely to get what one wants, nor is the Divine conceived as One who punishes those who have failed.[23] Sufferers are challenged to probe the depths of their pain as their experience of life is laid bare.

Ultimately, suffering offers the hopeful possibility of moving sufferers to an active and healthy acceptance of their pain. To do so, sufferers undergo metanoia as their attitudes change. *They accept what they do not understand.* "God's will be done" becomes their anthem. This acceptance, however, is distinct from unconditional submission, which is a passive resignation often sanctified by theology that comes from these representations. Sufferers come to acceptance by facing the purpose of suffering (inasmuch as it can be discerned). Acceptance includes the distinctive elements of protesting against suffering and battling to relieve it.

Thus sufferers' relation with God no longer depends upon the questioning, resentment, or even the outcome of any course of good or bad events. God's love for them flows without regard to any of these. They are invited to take a "leap of faith" and love God freely with mature unconditionality.[24] In this way God's goodness and power remain credible divine attributes, even though sufferers may still be in anguish.

As positive as this theology resounds, Depoortere notes its limitations. This perspective enriches the appreciation of suffering; again, it cannot be the final word. The inscrutability of God runs the risk of making suffering itself banal. It also presents the danger of being understood as condescension to humankind. Human suffering is relatively insignificant to the greatness of divine inscrutability. Recognition of this state of affairs by the human could lead to a loss of motivation to work against suffering, since all is ultimately inscrutable and in the hands of God. Understanding suffering as an unsolvable mystery can lead to indifferent resignation.

CONCLUSION

Each of these representations presents an image of the Divine that determines a particular manner of belief and its accompanying ethical and spiritual practices. They do not question, for example, the reality of a just Judge or of an inscrutable God, but rather a distorted application of these truths. Such distortions do not help the sufferer or correspond to proper appreciation of divine nature, particularly God's love. These portraits of the Divine can make sense of human suffering in ways that can be employed to justify pain by ascribing a divine origin to all suffering.[25] Thus suffering is given both an immediate and a transcendent purpose. Such an explanation offers a simple and accessible response to the complexity of human pain as well as to the true mystery of the Divine. Unconditional surrender would then be the appropriate but misguided response to such understanding.

Under normal circumstances one's faith is not troubled by the failings of these representations of the Divine, but all this

changes when a crisis occurs, such as the Juárez-Chihuahua feminicides. Here, adherence to these representations fails to provide comfort. Immeasurable anguish occurs when these divine
representations fail to offer adequate justification, for example,
in the loss of Julia Hernández-Hernández. The anguished believer
often responds to such a theological shortcoming by attempting to reconcile two or more divine attributes. While it may be
possible to combine omnipotence and justice, it is impossible to
combine omnipotence and love. Thus do all sufferers, from the
most humble layperson to the most sophisticated theologian, instinctively (even if secretly) ask: If God is omnipotent and loving,
why do the innocent suffer? Paula Bonilla-Flores, mother of the
slain Sagrario, reformulates this question with her assertions that
there *must* be justice in heaven, even if there is none in this world.

A God who would beget the kidnapping, torture, and murder
of hundreds of women for purposes of punishment or pedagogy is implausible. This suggests divine injustice and deficient
love. Offering this explanation to Julia Hernandez-Hernandez's
family would be a disgrace. The Juárez-Chihuahua feminicides
necessitate an appropriate response of inquiry, protest, and action—and ultimately cessation, not resignation, to the supposed
will of God.

Waiting to be found. *On March 16, 2011, nineteen-year-old Claudia Soto Castro left home, never to be seen again. The State's Attorney General Office is investigating.*

5

Apathy as a Response to Suffering

The opposite of love is not hate, it's indifference.

—Elie Wiesel

THE PHOTOGRAPH OF JAIME BAILLERES

Jaime Bailleres photographed a dead woman found in the desert outside of Juárez.[1] Only a haphazard attempt was made to hide her corpse. Her right foot and left leg protrude from a sandbank. She is still wearing her shoes: white with rubber soles meant for walking or standing all day, maybe on an assembly line. The spaces between the shoe straps form windows onto her brown skin. The heel of her left shoe is torn and bends backward like a loose flap of skin. Through her torn nylons I see the bruises that streak across her ankle. Sand covers the rest of her body.

The desecration of her body was simply the final step in the objectification of a human being used, dumped, and then tossed away. More than likely, her murderers had no fear of recourse.

I have just given my lecture on the Juárez-Chihuahua feminicides to a class of eighty university students. Along with Bailleres's photograph, I showed many of my own pictures, along with maps and charts. The room is silent; the students are genuinely stunned.

Questions come slowly at first, then more quickly. As I respond, I am waiting for a particular inquiry that always comes in one form or another.

A young man raises his hand. I point to him. "Yes, Joe?"

"Thousands of women work in these *maquiladoras*, right?"

"Yes, thousands."

"And the killing of these women started in 1993, correct?"

"That's when they found the first corpses," I reply. "But those bodies were already five to seven years old. No one really knows how long the murders have being going on. But 1993 is when people started paying attention and counting the women's murders."

"And aren't there thousands more killings in the drug war?"

"Yes, since Calderón's election in 2006, nearly forty thousand people have been killed in Mexico in drug-related violence."

"OK. There's something I don't get." Joe hesitates for a moment. "It may be inappropriate to say, but what are a couple of hundred of dead women out of the thousands of women that work in the *maquiladoras*? Aren't these only a few women in relation to the thousands of women who have worked in Juárez all these years? Couldn't you say that these killings are just an occupational hazard of working in Juárez? I don't mean these killings aren't tragic or anything like that. But I don't get why this is such a big deal."

Joe must be given credit for the honesty of his inquiry. His discomfort was indication enough that he understood his question to be loaded.

Joe's response to the killings rings true. It is remarkably similar to the line of questions friends and colleagues ask when they learn of my area of research. I have found that initial interest and even fascination abounds regarding the hundreds of missing and dead women. "So, who's killing the women?" I am asked initially, as if I am the author of a great whodunit.

"There's no simple answer," I respond. "In fact, the situation in Juárez is quite complex."

"But who are the actual killers?"

A cat's interest in a dangled string wanes once the string is lying still at its paws. Similarly, my questioners' attention usually fades when they realize that these murders are much more than just a mysterious serial killing—and it is gone completely once they grasp that the culpability for the killings extends outward to the global economy and the international narcotics trade. Mere consumption of consumer goods, including the use of illegal drugs, indirectly implicates us all.

But more centrally, we are all implicated in the Juárez-Chihuahua feminicides by our passive response.

APATHY: A SPIRITUAL MALADY OF THE NOONDAY DEMON

In theological/spiritual traditions, apathy is treated under the classification of *acedia* or *indifference*.[2] Ancient monastic authors such as Evagrius Ponticus, John Cassian, and Gregory the Great have left us detailed treatments of the indifference that they consider to be a vice. In the fourth century Ponticus colorfully personified this spiritual malady as "the noonday demon," stating that this demon "causes the most serious trouble of all."[3]

According to Ponticus, the demon seduces its subject with the inability to commit to spiritual values and is characterized by carelessness, unconcern, and sadness. The consequence of chronic apathy is a state of acedia, a pervading spiritual emptiness. Ponticus describes the demon's desire for a monk to lapse into acedia and strikes during the heat of the day when the monk is hungry and fatigued and therefore vulnerable to the suggestion that his commitment to a life of prayer is not worth the effort.[4]

This noonday reference suggests that acedia and its counterpart, apathy, approach openly, not cloaked in the darkness that evil is generally presumed to wear. The demon is accepted as an afternoon guest; while enjoying this hospitality, the demon seizes its host. Apathy is therefore a *spiritual* malady.

In the classic theological tradition acedia stood on its own as the eighth deadly sin. Later it was grouped logically with the third deadly sin, sloth. This more familiar categorization offers insight into the moral and spiritual core of apathy. Sloth is much more than mere idleness, laziness, or aversion to work; it is a full lack of desire that constitutes the sin of spiritual sloth. It is the absence of caring, indicating a severe malady of a deadened spirit.

Ultimately, sloth is the failure to love.[5] Thus, one of the greatest of human crimes, the sin of omission, is the consequence of apathy. Generally speaking, the grand paradox of apathetic people is that they hold no malice against others; they simply don't care. Apathy also prevents spirited protest against, questioning of, or movement toward the alleviation of suffering. Thus we see in the apathetic person and society an illustration of a classic dictum: the opposite of love is not hate but indifference.

For a modern consideration of acedia I turn to psychologist Rollo May. While May studied at Union Theological Seminary in the 1930s, he was befriended and influenced by Paul Tillich, one of his instructors. Yet the turning point in May's life came when he faced death from tuberculosis. He spent three years recovering in a sanatorium, where he found inspiration in the writings of Søren Kierkegaard.

May's *Love and Will*, which enjoyed vast popularity in the late 1960s, is no less relevant today. The leading existential psychologist of his time, May also demonstrates a deep appreciation for spiritual values often echoing the wisdoms of Ponticus. May argues that deepest psychological healing comes from the capacity to believe, sustain, hope, and learning to love.

May understands apathy not only as limited to an individual psychological and spiritual illness but also as a plague endemic to modern society. Apathy is a state of *affectivelessness,* a "want of feeling," a "lack of passion, emotion, or excitement."[6] May associates the *sadness* spiritual masters describe as indicative of apathy not only with a state of depression but also with a deeper infirmity:

a *spiritual void* inherent to the apathetic state. For May, apathy is the inability of either the individual or society to feel, which creates distance from the suffering of self and others.

May understands apathy as a defense mechanism against the anxiety and overstimulation of modern society. In this, we can see that May was influenced by the notion of apathy called shell shock, which was first observed in surviving soldiers from World War I. A more developed understanding of such stress is now referred to as post-traumatic stress disorder. May applies this understanding to the noise, crowds, assembly lines, crowded freeways, and stressful work and home environments that assault and batter us each day. He observes that anyone who has ever experienced rush hour on the New York subway system, "with its cacophonous din and hordes of anonymous humanity, cannot begrudge the disengaged and worn-out commuters their defensive strategy of detachment."[7] Apathy also has less complicated manifestations, such as simple boredom, listlessness at work, or a lack of desire for social interactions.

Unfortunately, apathy as a defense only augments large and small traumas, leading to further emptiness; it leaves us less able to defend ourselves, less able to survive.[8] Eventually, apathetic persons can become weary of their own indifference but oblivious to either its cause or cure. More severe apathy can manifest as a profound lack of feeling or as a despairing sense that nothing really matters. Since despair can turn into destructiveness as an attempt to acquire any feeling at all, apathy has the potential to explode into violence.[9]

Dorothee Soelle shares May's view of apathy as a malady rampant in modern society. Her treatment of apathy takes the form of pointed social critique. In her search for an appropriate response to human suffering, Soelle observes that the most common reaction to suffering is no response at all. Individuals—even entire societies—easily ignore suffering in their midst. Soelle specifically addresses the apathy that rises from middle-class

indulgence and self-satisfaction, aiming her critique at "the apathetic people in the industrial nations. . . . The apathetic ideal
bears the imprint of the middle-class consciousness."[10]

For Soelle, apathy begins with the denial of one's own pain and
is exacerbated by the belief that a suffering-free state of being is
possible. People become so preoccupied with avoiding suffering
that they end up feeling nothing whatsoever and caring for no
one—even themselves. This flight to eliminate pain results in
the avoidance of human relationships, or at least the tendency
to engage others only superficially. Soelle contends that a per
son numb to pain no longer has the capacity to perceive reality.
Apathy results in a self-inflicted sort of blindness that Soelle finds
"possible in a society in which a banal optimism prevails, in which
it is self-evident that suffering doesn't occur." This does not mean
that the apathetic person does not suffer. Quite the contrary. The
most disturbing part of this blindness applies to the individual's
lack of awareness of his or her own suffering. The person either
represses it or just puts up with it.[11]

A consequence of repression is that authentic passions such
as joy and pain are reduced to distant apparitions. "Painless satisfaction guarantees the attainment of quiet stagnation," Soelle
says, because to feel pain would open the affective floodgates to
the host of other unwanted human emotions.[12] The long-term
consequence of this insensitivity is a deficiency of compassion
and a moral callousness that naturally results in a low level of
responsiveness to the suffering of others.

Lack of compassion may be selective, with certain individuals,
groups, genders, or races falling outside an individual's or society's domain of caring—even when the sufferers are immediately
present. Soelle holds both individuals and society responsible for
individual apathy, even though part of apathy's nature is that the
host is unaware of its malignant presence.

On April 18, 2010, Hugo Alfredo Tale-Yax, a homeless man
in New York, was stabbed while rescuing a Queens woman
from a knife-wielding attacker. The homeless hero lay on the

sidewalk in a pool of his own blood for more than two hours while twenty-five people walked past him. This shocking incident was caught on a surveillance video and aired repeatedly on the national news. Some of the passersby gawked at Hugo. One stopped to shake him. Another paused just long enough to take a photograph. Hugo bled to death there on the sidewalk because no one bothered to call 911.[13] The incident was a disturbingly ironic inversion of the Good Samaritan drama, with the hero saving a life only to become a tragic victim of human indifference.

Hugo's death brings to mind a similar story of indifference and inaction: the 1964 murder in New York of Kitty Genovese. While some details of the original *New York Times* report have come into question, the story of the inaction of Genovese's neighbors while she was murdered over the course of a half-hour inspired research into the nature of what later became known as the *bystander effect* or the *Genovese syndrome*, a phenomenon in which bystanders offer no assistance to individuals in crisis.[14]

In a series of classic studies, researchers Bibb Latané and John M. Darley found that the number of people who stand idly by when someone is in danger might be key to understanding the bystanders' behavior. "Although it seems obvious that the more people who watch an emergency, the more likely it is that someone will help, what really happens is exactly the reverse. *The presence of other people serves to inhibit the impulse to help.*" The presence of others actually "inhibits action" and can prevent bystanders from "even showing concern." The bystanders' primary focus is how they will be perceived by other bystanders, resulting in those present "try[ing] to maintain a calm demeanor, or unruffled front."[15] Myriad psychological and social factors interplay in the bystander effect. Apathy is one of these, and it cannot be dismissed.

Both Soelle and May voice their concerns at how the media contribute to both societal and individual apathy. Soelle contends that "walls are erected between the experiencing subject and reality. One learns about suffering of others only indirectly—one sees starving children on TV—and this kind of suffering of others is characteristic of our entire perception."[16] Meanwhile, May understands this onslaught of modern communication as a potential psychological danger: "In the alienated states of mass communication, the average citizen knows dozens of TV personalities who come smiling into his living room of an evening—but he himself is never known. In this state of alienation and anonymity, painful for anyone to bear, the average person may well have fantasies which hover on the edge of real pathology."[17] As Soelle remarks, "People stand before suffering like those who are color-blind, incapable of perception without any sensibility."[18] Incidents such as the deaths of Hugo Tale-Yax and Kitty Genovese indicate how serious this blindness has become in modern society.

Soelle's critique of apathy identifies tangible social causes of its contemporary escalation, and her focus is a modern world where apathy has unnaturally quenched all perception of human suffering. These causes of apathy might well serve as an anti-expression of the beatitudes:

- *We have everything we need.* Shortage of essential commodities has all but been eliminated.
- *We need not see the suffering before us.* Private prosperity obscures public poverty, helping to shield people from being conscious of human suffering.
- *We can escape the complications that come with loving others.* Greater social mobility means that unwanted relations easily can be eliminated from our lives.
- *We no longer need to feel.* Opiates of every kind and other means of producing numbness through overstimulation allow us to forget suffering and eliminate psychological distress.[19]

Since May's time societal overstimulation has skyrocketed with increased populations, a greater frequency of violence, and ever-larger arrays of technological devices that keep us constantly updated, entertained, and distracted. Thus May's mid-twentieth-century caution concerning prolonged states of escapist apathy becomes a prophetic herald for our time: "The longer the situation goes unmet, the more apathy is prolonged; and it sooner or later becomes a character state."[20] It is an echo of the warning Ponticus voiced sixteen centuries earlier: "The noonday demon is accustomed to embrace the entire soul and oppress the spirit."[21]

INDIFFERENCE LEADS TO VIOLENCE

Reflecting on his experience with his clients, May concludes that sex has become so available that the only way to preserve any center is to learn to have intercourse without committing oneself. Soelle makes a similar observation. Even marriage is no guarantee of true involvement or openness to vulnerability, she points out, but can be perceived as temporary, enjoyed until unbearable, then swiftly dissolved by a divorce that leaves as few scars as possible.[22] May and Soelle are convinced that such profound detachment from committing oneself is a step toward a slow and self-inflicted morbidity. "To desire freedom from pain means to desire death," says Soelle.[23] May likens the consequences of apathy to an acting out of the Freudian "death instinct," although May understands it as a gradual letting go of involvement until one finally finds that life itself has gone by.[24]

People cannot live in such an empty condition for very long; the nebulous torment of non-feeling is too much to endure. Humans long for some feeling or experience that offers proof they are alive. If people do not grow and work toward personal and professional goals, they do not merely stagnate; their unrealized potentialities turn into morbidity and despair—and perhaps to destructive activities.[25] An inner void impels individuals to vain and usually destructive attempts to fill themselves from without. Alcohol and other drugs, sex, and various other types of anesthetization are readily available for that purpose.

But such misguided efforts do not satisfactorily displace empathy. Rather, they leave the individual even more estranged and depersonalized, stimulated but emotionless, living but spiritually dead. In extreme cases this lack of responsiveness leads to violence and can reach a pathological dimension. Sociopaths are individuals who apparently lack certain norms of feeling. They may show indifference to the suffering of others, even the suffering that the sociopaths themselves may have inflicted, whether directly or indirectly. May posits a dialectical relationship between apathy and violence; that is, living in apathy provokes violence and violence promotes apathy.

> Violence is the ultimate destructive substitute which surges in to fill the vacuum where there is no relatedness. . . . When inward life dries up, when feeling decreases and apathy increases, when one cannot affect or even genuinely touch another person, violence flares up as a daimonic necessity for contact, a mad drive forcing touch in the most direct way possible. This is one aspect of the well-known relationship between sexual feelings and crimes of violence. To inflict pain and torture at least proves that one can affect somebody. The mood of the anonymous person is, if I cannot affect or touch anybody, I can at least shock you into something, force you into some passion through wounds and pain; I shall at least make sure we both feel something, and I shall force you to see and know that I am also here![26]

The sexual molestations that characterize the Juárez-Chihuahua feminicides seem only one example of the deadened sensitivities of the perpetrators. Yet we must not overlook the fact that many of the murdered women died by strangulation or multiple stab wounds, followed by the mutilation of their corpses, which were subsequently discarded in a manner that characterized them literally as garbage. That this has recurred hundreds of times without greater outrage reveals pathological callousness, both individual and societal.

Given the relationship between apathy and violence, we can ask if the perpetrators of these feminicides are themselves so overstimulated by the violent world around them that their self-defense response (as May would characterize their state) leads them to inflict pain on others so they themselves might feel. Although these are only conjectures, May's theories cannot be dismissed.

CONCLUSION

Interest in the killings does not usually go deeper than the whodunit level and is not unrelated to the logic presented in the *maquiloca* and *maquiladora* discourses to construct an acceptable rationale for dismissing the suffering, disappearance, and murdering of these women. Such apathy denies the women's humanity. Thus the women are revictimized by being again objectified, categorized, and finally forgotten. They are used and dumped one last time, receiving no justice, spurring no efforts to stop the killings. Although masked, all of these responses send a clear message of apathy: These women are not worthy of worry.

The overarching issue concerning the Juárez-Chihuahua feminicides is that the U.S. and Mexican reactions have been dominated by a lack of legitimate concern. The consequence of this indifference is the lack of constructive measures to bring an end to the killings. And so women continue to die. Does a sense of defused responsibility among millions of bystanders on both sides of the border let us all off the hook? Another cautionary lesson can be found in the indifference to the missing and dead women. May and Soelle insist that such apathy eventually takes a toll on those who look away. When we turn away from human pain, we deaden our own capacity to feel. Denial of another's suffering negates not only that person's humanity but also our own. And so each of us must take responsibility for offering or not offering our attention. Otherwise, we will become the subjects of our own deficient compassion and moral callousness.

A missing daughter. Norma Laguna Cabral raises a banner of protest accompanied by two of her daughters. Her other daughter, Idali Juache Laguna, disappeared on February 23, 2010.

6

Is There a Suffering God?

I don't know what it means for God to suffer.

—Rabbi Harold S. Kushner[1]

At the heart of the suffering of the woman-killings in Juárez are two key theological questions. First, what is God's relationship with the suffering of these women? Is God a distant observer of their suffering? Or is God present in their suffering? At the crux of this question, is an omnipotent God subject to pain? The second concern deals with senseless suffering. We are most often able to make some sense out of suffering when we ultimately learn from it or it brings some positive change into our lives; thus, we attribute some saving purpose to this pain. Yet what are we to make of senseless suffering like the woman-killings in Juárez? How do we respond to affliction that offers no apparent redemptive meaning?

The question whether God is subject to suffering refers to the idea of a God of pathos—a God that can feel pain. Within this question lives an age-old theological question that has become very important today. Pondering it returns us to discussions of Holocaust events that have challenged traditional theologies of the suffering of Jews and Christians alike. Theological understandings differ vastly on this subject. Post-Shoah thinking about

God's relation to human suffering plays an essential part in formulating our perspectives on the senseless suffering in Juárez.

In this chapter I offer a brief overview of contemporary theological discussion about whether God is present in senseless suffering. As in the other chapters I begin with a narrative, but instead of a first-person account, I recount here one of most renowned narratives of the twentieth century, Elie Wiesel's memoir *Night*, which offers an instance of suffering and inhumanity indicative of the twentieth-century experience.

ELIE WIESEL'S *NIGHT*

In *Night*'s most famous scene, a young Wiesel and thousands of other prisoners stand before the gallows of the Jewish concentration camp known as Buna. They are there to witness the hanging of two men and a young boy.

> All eyes were on the child. He was lividly pale, almost calm, biting his lips. The gallows threw its shadow over him.
>
> The three victims mounted together onto the chairs.
>
> The three necks were placed at the same moment within the nooses.
>
> "Long live liberty!" cried the two adults.
>
> But the child was silent.
>
> "Where is God? Where is He?" someone behind me asked.
>
> At the sign from the head of the camp, the three chairs tipped over.
>
> Total silence throughout the camp. On the horizon the sun was setting.
>
> "Bare your heads!" yelled the head of the camp. His voice was raucous. We were weeping.
>
> "Cover your heads!"

Then the march past began. The two adults were no longer alive. Their tongues hung swollen, blue-tinged. But the third rope was still moving; being so light, the child was still alive. . . .

For more than half an hour he stayed there, struggling between life and death, dying in slow agony under our eyes. And we had to look him full in the face. He was still alive when I passed in front of him. His tongue was still red, his eyes not yet glazed.

Behind me, I heard the same man asking:

"Where is God now?"

And I heard a voice within me answer him:

"Where is He? Here He is—He is hanging here on this gallows."[2]

How do we begin to understand this scene? The adolescent Wiesel was not a trained theologian; instead, he was schooled in the death camps of Auschwitz, Buchenwald, and Buna. His report of the men's responses provides some initial insight to these deaths—the boy's in particular. First are the two men about to be hanged, who shout, "Long live liberty!" Their death becomes a statement of defiance and resistance.[3] Then there is the boy, who has neither committed a crime nor voiced any political consciousness; he is simply an innocent victim of suffering. An onlooker who stands before the dying child poses the theodical question three times, "Where is God now?" chiding the other prisoners with his remark. His question focuses on God's seeming abandonment rather than expressing compassion for the boy. He asks for justification of God's inaction rather than divine assistance. The onlooker announces the apparent triumph of human cruelty, instead of offering hope, and suggests his own state of despair and atheistic rebellion. Last, we have Wiesel's famous interior comment, "Where is He? Here He is—He is hanging here on this gallows." Generally, Christian scholars such as Dorothee Soelle interpret this moment as an echo of a divine presence, perhaps even Christ's crucifixion, thus affirming the divine suffering present in the anguish of humankind.[4]

Interestingly, some scholars interpret Wiesel's comment as being in the same vein as the onlooker's: an expression of atheism, an empty death of an innocent child rescued by neither divine intervention nor presence. Other scholars, including Sarah K. Pinnock, walk a middle ground, suggesting it is a moment both of atheism and faith.[5] Johann Baptist Metz offers still another stance regarding Christian responses to the Holocaust, one with which I am in accord. As Metz says, "Holocaust victims must be given authority with respect to the religious interpretation of this catastrophe."[6]

Wiesel's narrative of one of the most well-known examples of the horror of the Holocaust sets the stage for this chapter. This event rightly ignited twentieth-century secular and religious thinkers from every tradition in their reconsideration of the theodical question. Old rationales for human suffering, such as divine punishment for sin, rang not only hollow but also overtly offensive in response to the killing of six million Jews. As Wiesel's scene provokes a plurality of theological interpretations of God's relationship to the men's suffering, so too contemporary theological discussion about the notion of a suffering God varies with regard to key points in Wiesel's narrative. Is the God of pathos present in the dying men, and in the innocent boy in particular? And if God suffers with them, then what is the nature of this divine presence? The Catholic theological tradition has long maintained that God cannot suffer directly. Essentially, this means that God is subject neither to feelings nor to change.

To explore the post-Shoah notion of a God of pathos, I begin with a survey of various sources from the Hellenic to the Enlightenment periods. I then offer an overview of three representative post-Shoah theologians, Jürgen Moltmann, Dorothee Soelle, and Johann Baptist Metz.

GOD IN THE HELLENISTIC TRADITION

God as *impassible* refers to an unfeeling God, one not subject to suffering, pain, and harm. Scholars of theology, including Richard Bauckham, have discussed how the Greek fathers took this view for granted and were suspicious of any theological tendency that might threaten the essential impassibility that they considered the definitive aspect of the divine nature.[7] This view emerged from several key philosophic principles that require further explication.

The idea that the Divine cannot be affected by something from the outside means that God cannot suffer because God is absolutely self-sufficient, self-determining, and independent. Pathos in our understanding of pain or calamity includes the passions, which are all emotions from extreme joy to extreme suffering. The Greeks viewed suffering as an experience that comes upon a person; to suffer is to be acted upon against one's will. Therefore, to suffer is to become a passive victim. Implicit in suffering is vulnerability and weakness. This argument is operative in that it recognizes that being moved by emotion (such as desire or fear) is being acted upon, affected from the outside, as opposed to being self-determining.[8] To the Greeks, then, the vulnerability that comprises the affective life was contrary to the very idea of omnipotence. Since God can neither be acted upon nor be weak, God must be devoid of emotions.

The Greek view of divine immutability further supported the idea of the unfeeling God. Suffering involves temporality, inconstancy, and matter—features of the material world, not the spiritual realm of God. To the Greeks, God was atemporal and incorporeal, absolute and perfect, beyond change. The affective life, with its emotions and their dynamic variations, was incompatible with the Greeks' notion of God.

The Greeks perceived this understanding of God positively. God's benevolence could not be swayed by passion, and God's eternal blessedness was unassailable. The Greek fathers completely trusted in God's love for the world.[9] Bauckham explains that this love was "a benevolent attitude and activity, not a feeling, and not a relationship in which he can be *affected* by what he loves."[10] Bauckham notes that

> a further implication of the doctrine of divine *apatheia* is very important: it has as its corollary *apatheia* as a human ideal. This occurs, in varying degrees and forms, in the Greek philosophical schools and in the Fathers, but the general Greek tendency was to see essential human nature as self-determining reason, which as such resembles God. Ideally, the emotions ought to be subject to the reason, but in fact through them the flesh and the material world are able to influence and sway the reason, resulting in sin and suffering.[11]

DEISM: THE ABSENTEE LANDLORD

Seventeenth- and eighteenth-century deism iterated the idea of the non-feeling God. Signifying religious heterodoxy, deism's numerous strains contain both a philosophy and a belief that rationally arrives at proof of God.[12] Deism asserts that God created the world but, after doing so, exercised no providential control over creation or its inhabitants—hence the analogy of God as an absentee landlord.[13] It is difficult, however, to conceive of a God who would leave divine creation to its own devices while simultaneously engaging in a complex historical process of divine self-revelation. For what purpose? Thus, while affirming the existence of a divine creator, deism denies divine revelation, therefore arguing that human reason alone is sufficient to arrive at a correct moral and religious life.

Various theodical schools battle for some coherence of the Divine's three attributes: omniscience, omnipotence, and omnibenevolence. The central concern occupying theodicy is how to justify the existence of human suffering in light of a God that is all powerful, all knowing, and all benevolent. If this three-pronged description of God is accurate, then God must have no interest in redressing suffering.

THE BIBLICAL EMANCIPATION

Beginning in the nineteenth century and gaining momentum in the twentieth was a Christian movement to "de-Hellenize" scripture and return to a sense of continuity between Christianity and Judaism. This modern theological trend shifted the scriptural understanding of God from the Greek categories of theism, particularly the divine attributes of immutability and impassibility.[14] The philosophic conceptualizations of God that influenced the Christian theological tradition differ radically from those of the sacred scriptures. The God of Hebrew scripture establishes a covenant with the Hebrews, forming them into God's people. This covenant is founded upon a personal relationship: "I will be your God and you will be my people" (Lev 26:12).

In this tradition divine emotion plays an indispensable role in God's salvation plan. God displays wrath and punishes sinners; God forgives, heals, and saves; God acts with tenderness and compassion. In 1936, Abraham Heschel, in his pioneering study of the prophets, developed a theology of divine pathos. "The most exalted idea applied to God is not infinite wisdom, infinite power, but infinite concern," Heschel writes. "He who does not live on others, cares for others. . . . In order to conceive of God not as an onlooker but as a participant, to conceive of man not as an idea in the mind of God but as a concern, the category of divine pathos is an indispensable implication."[15]

TWENTIETH-CENTURY THEOLOGIES OF SUFFERING

A consideration of a contemporary theology of suffering would be incomplete without a contextualization of twentieth-century developments in the understanding of a suffering God. The suffering caused by two world wars, the Holocaust, and global poverty spawned theological inquiry within the tradition at large. Modern thinkers reflected on firsthand experiences of human cruelty, destruction, and death, searching for sensible, comprehensive, and sympathetic theological responses. While surveying these theologies, it is important to consider the Catholic theological tradition on suffering, while at the same time responding to contemporary concerns that differ on fundamental theological tenets.

Of the many who explored the modern question of suffering, three representative thinkers of the Christian traditions illuminate a discussion of God and senseless suffering. In what follows, I explore the arguments of renowned Protestant theologian Jürgen Moltmann in *The Crucified God* (1973) and *The Trinity and the Kingdom of God* (1981); Lutheran Dorothee Soelle's *Suffering*; and Catholic theologian of suffering Johann Baptist Metz's *Faith in History and Society*.

Moltmann's The Crucified God

Jesus' death on the cross is at the center of all Christian theology. For Moltmann, it is an opening to addressing the notion of the suffering of God. Since the crucifixion is the decisive event of divine suffering, Moltmann argues that God's suffering in the

person of Jesus Christ cannot be confined to the cross, strategically avoiding two early theological premises, since discredited:
theopascitism, the sixth-century doctrine holding that Christ
had only one nature, which was his suffering on the cross; and
patripassianism, which denied the distinct person of the Trinity
by claiming that God the Father had become incarnate and suffered for the salvation of humankind.[16]

Moltmann refers to "a trinitarian event of the suffering of
God," by which he means that all three members of the Trinity
participated in Jesus' suffering. In his view the crucifixion was
an event of suffering *internal* to God, that is to say, it was an
"inner-trinitarian tension and relationship."[17] Moltmann distinguishes the different ways in which the Father, Son, and Spirit
participated in the crucifixion.[18] Moltmann's point here is that
"the grief of the Father . . . is just as important as the death of
the Son."[19] Thus, Moltmann claims that the Father's participation
in the suffering of Jesus was twofold: the Father delivers the Son
to death on the cross, an act of "paternal deliverance" that Moltmann understands as the "total and inextricable abandonment
of Jesus by both his God and Father,"[20] and out of love for the
Son, the Father endures the anguish of the Son's abandonment
and death.[21] Through this separation, the Holy Spirit remains an
expression of mutual love between the Father and the Son. Yet as
a consequence of the Father and Son separation, the Holy Spirit
is poured forth to reach humankind in need.

This theological posture allows Moltmann to argue that the
crucifixion can be addressed *only* in trinitarian terms, because
if this event encompasses "God's own trinitarian being," it determines the Christian doctrine of God. "What happens on the
cross manifests the relationship of Jesus the Son to the Father,
and vice versa, along with the movement of the Spirit to us. The
cross stands at the heart of the trinitarian being of God: it divides
and conjoins the persons in their relationship to each other and
portrays them in a specific way."[22]

To accompany his theology of the cross, Moltmann also develops a particular understanding of human suffering. The crucifixion is an expression of God's love for those he understands as
godless,[23] and he refers to "godlessness" and "godforsakenness."[24]
For Moltmann, abandonment by God made Jesus godless; abandonment by his Father made him godforsaken. Jesus shares this
dual desolation in the suffering of the godless and godforsaken of
the world. According to Moltmann, "Though they [the suffering
of the world] are godless, they are not godforsaken, precisely
because God has abandoned his own Son and has delivered him
up for them."[25] With his death cry, Jesus embodies the plight of
godlessness and godforsakenness: "My God, my God, why have
you forsaken me?" (Mk 15:35). In these words, Moltmann hears
a potent echo that resounds with far more than a death lament
or poignant quotation of the second verse of Psalm 22. Jesus' cry
takes the form of a question that voices a protest against suffering. In this definitive moment of salvation Moltmann hears Jesus
questioning the manner of God's righteousness in the world.
Why has God delivered up his own Son? What is God's relationship to human suffering? Why has God forsaken those who are
faithful to him?

As his dying legacy, Jesus questions the manner of God's righteousness in the world while simultaneously taking up humanity's
protest against suffering. When humanity cries out in suffering,
Moltmann understands those beckoning in pain reiterating Jesus' anguished laments: "Anyone who cries out to God in this
suffering echoes the death-cry of the dying Christ, the Son of
God." For Moltmann, there is in this shared experience a new
divine-human solidarity that has been forged because "the cross is
not just a revelation of the divine sympathy for those who suffer,
but an act of divine solidarity with the 'godless and godforsaken,'
in which the Son of God actually enters their situation of godforsakenness."[26] In his final moments, the dying Jesus is not the
incomprehensible God "set over" humankind who inflicts suffering;

rather, he shares in the suffering of the world as a "human God who cries with [the sufferer] and intercedes for him with his cross where man in his torment is dumb."[27]

Alfred North Whitehead, among others, has argued that if Jesus were only "a fellow-sufferer who understands," then the problem of suffering would not be alleviated but exacerbated. The sufferer receives no real consolation in knowing that God is a helpless victim in the face of the world's suffering.[28]

Moltmann responds to such criticism by arguing two points. First, divine solidarity helps those who suffer because it transforms the "character of the suffering; it heals the deepest pain in human suffering, which is godforsakenness."[29] According to Moltmann,

> the suffering is overcome by suffering, and wounds are healed by wounds. For the suffering in suffering is a lack of love, and the wounds in wounds are the abandonment, and the powerlessness in pain is unbelief. And therefore the suffering of abandonment is overcome by the suffering of love, which is not afraid of what is sick and ugly, but accepts it and takes it to itself in order to heal it. Through his own abandonment by God, the crucified Christ brings God to those who are abandoned by God. Through his suffering he brings salvation to those who suffer.[30]

Second, Moltmann does not isolate the cross, "let alone make it something absolute in itself." Rather, he focuses on the resurrection with unbounded hope, because "without the resurrection, the cross really is quite simply a tragedy and nothing more than that."[31] For Moltmann, the resurrection is God's promise of liberation to all of those suffering humans who have tasted the gall of godlessness and godforsakenness: "If we follow the testimony of the first Christian witnesses, the depth of the agony of fear which Christ experienced on the cross is far and away surpassed by the sense of expansion in his resurrection."[32]

Soelle's **Suffering**

Dorothee Soelle's response to suffering emerges from her experience of World War II Germany. Her brother died in battle; her family hid a Jew in their home; and with the horrific disclosure that Nazis had murdered millions of Jews, Soelle felt a sense of "ineradicable shame."[33] Undoubtedly, the Holocaust pushed Soelle's thinking far beyond the traditional Lutheranism of her upbringing. She sought new responses to suffering from a culture that seemed indifferent to human pain—even its own. Even forty years after the publication of *Suffering*, Soelle's critique of the Lutheran theology of suffering still raises Christian eyebrows in its provocative presentation of bold theological challenges.

Soelle has held fast to fundamental convictions that God does in fact suffer and that God is present in human suffering. Her understanding of that divine presence in human suffering evolved in three stages.[34] First, she questioned classic theism's premise of an omnipotent God; second, she explored the powerless crucified God who offers an example of love; and third, she pondered the crucified and resurrected Christ who triumphs over suffering. Soelle continually moved toward a more mystical understanding of God's relationship with humankind's suffering, relying on such mystics as John of the Cross, Edith Stein, and even Bernard of Clairvaux.[35]

For the purposes of understanding the Juárez-Chihuahua woman-killings, Soelle's first stage is most relevant. Her bold outcry of rebellious theology crafted in a post-Shoah reality reacted contemptuously to traditional Lutheran presuppositions of suffering. Soelle's critique of Moltmann's theology of the cross is founded on his complex Father-Son-Spirit dynamic. For Soelle, the trinitarian affliction comes at the expense of portraying God in a contradictory and dualistic relationship where Jesus suffers at the hands of his own Father. For Soelle, this means that the God who suffers is the same God who causes suffering.

She expands this fundamental critique to the whole of Molt-mann's theology. Moltmann has crafted a theology of a suffering Christ whose pain is aligned with the poor but then emphasizes that it is God the Father who inflicts this suffering upon the af-flicted. Such logic flies in the face of one of Soelle's fundamen-tal tenets: an omnipotent God. From Soelle's perspective, the omnipotent God creates a dangerous conundrum: God is both the origin and cause of suffering, as well the One called upon to relieve suffering. Soelle is dissatisfied with any theology that sees God operating from a position of power rather than compassion. She says of Moltmann's theology, "This intention, this passion for suffering, is weakened and softened through the theological system that transmits it."[36]

Another of Soelle's early and provocative discourses was her questioning of the Christian theology of suffering that is employed to vindicate divine power though human weakness. Soelle argues that from the theistic perspective, once God's omnipotence and uniqueness are presupposed, the Divine is re-lieved of any accountability for suffering, and instead individuals or humanity as a whole are held responsible for misery by right of human weakness.[37] In such a state of affairs, suffering's intent is to break human pride and demonstrate human weakness, thus exploiting human dependency on God. Soelle sees the concept of sickness—indeed, any human weakness—as often used for these religious ends.

Soelle also questions what she calls "Christian masochism," a Christian's willingness to suffer because God caused or willed it. Soelle takes an intrepid stand against this "unconditional sur-render," which manifests as acceptance of suffering as a test sent by God, punishment for sin, or a refinement process (through which humans are purified).[38]

But if unconditional submission is the normative response to suffering, then the sufferer is unable to make any real sense of pain. If suffering is simply accepted as the will of God, then this pain goes unchallenged, and consequently, real measures for relieving or eliminating unnecessary suffering never occur. Unchecked suffering has the potential to spawn hopelessness not only from a distorted notion of the Divine who inflicts punishment but also as a consequence of overwhelming misery. Such crippling confusion and pain can ultimately result in atheism or despair.[39] Soelle's preoccupation—and one of her most important contributions to the discussion of suffering—is the recognition that a theology of suffering must include questioning and protest. On this point Moltmann and Soelle agree, as both dismiss blind acceptance of suffering in favor of questioning and protest.[40]

As challenging as Soelle's theology is, she does not see unconditional submission as the worst possible response to human suffering. She dares to take her thinking a step further: If the Divine is all power and does not act randomly, and if God sends suffering as a consequence of sin, then this suggests that God must in some way find pleasure in human suffering. Thus Soelle provocatively refers to the "sadist God," describing a theology of suffering that can be "insensitive to human misery." Such a theology contradicts Christianity's fundamental premise of love, expressing "contempt of humanity,"[41] and sin, not love, becomes the religion's driving force. "Brutality and salvation become brothers," she says. "Suffering serves to teach of obedience."[42]

Apart from her critique of past theologies of suffering, Soelle advances her theology of a God who is vulnerable to suffering, a God present in human pain. With regard to the Holocaust, Soelle holds that the God of pathos was present in these victims. She writes, "In his emptied, abased form, God shares the suffering of his people in exile, in prison, in martyrdom. . . . God suffers where his people suffer. God must be delivered from pain." With the age-old theological method of considering who God is not, she writes, "God is no executioner—and no almighty spectator (which would amount to the same thing). God is not the mighty

tyrant. Between the sufferer and the one who causes the suffering, between the victim and the executioner . . . God is on the
side of the sufferer."[43]

What God *is*, Soelle fervently argues, is a God aligned with
human suffering: "God, whatever people make of this world,
is on the side of the sufferer. God is on the side of the victim."
And with the Holocaust victim in mind, Soelle offers her own
Christian understanding of Holocaust victims: "Every single one
of the six million Jews was God's beloved son."[44]

Metz's Faith in History and Society

Born in Germany in 1928, Johann Baptist Metz was sixteen
at the end of World War II when he was called to the final draft
by the Third Reich. During his service Metz experienced a
life-changing event. After couriering a message, he returned to
headquarters to discover that all of the other men in his company
had been attacked and killed. Metz recalls this trauma:

> I found all my comrades dead. . . . I saw only the lifeless
> faces of my comrades, those same comrades which whom
> I had but days before shared my childhood fears and my
> youthful laughter. I remember nothing but a soundless cry.
> . . . Over and over again, just this silent cry. And up until
> today I see myself so. Behind this memory all my childhood
> dreams have vanished.[45]

Thus did irreconcilable affliction enter Metz's life, forever turning his thinking toward the meaning of senseless suffering.[46] After
the war, he began his studies for the Roman Catholic priesthood
and was ordained in 1953. Metz was entrusted with the chair in
fundamental theology at the Catholic faculty at the University
of Münster until his retirement in 1993.[47]

A Catholic theologian, Metz has various influences. Seminal
to Metz's thinking is his German rural Catholic background,

with its intense and conflicted rapport with the Enlightenment, which still dominated German thinking of his time. Next, his long intellectual and personal relationship with Karl Rahner, of which Metz reflected, "[from him,] I have learned everything I know. . . . [and] from whom we continue to learn even when we have to contradict him."[48] Yet it was Ernst Bloch and Walter Benjamin who were crucial interlocutors in Metz's parting with Rahner's transcendental Thomism. Metz made a decisive shift from the speculation and *theoria* to emphasize practical reason and *praxis*;[49] in plain terms, Metz simply could not distance his theological reflections from the outcries of twentieth-century human suffering. Therefore, while it may at first come as a surprise to find that Metz sustains an intellectual relationship with Marxism, particularly precarious because of its critique of religion, like Soelle (among others), Metz adapts the Marxist critique of the middle class's apathy toward the poor and suffering, pleading for the conversion of their consciousness.

Metz's own war experiences also bonded him to the Jews, particularly Holocaust victims and survivors, in their struggle to make sense out of the shared horrors of their generation. Furthermore, Metz's work reexamines the relationship between Christianity and Judaism, as well as Hellenization and Christianity. Finally, world oppression and the disparity between first-world and third-world realities captured Metz's keen political awareness and theologizing, leading him to join in liberation theology's proclamation of the fundamental option for the poor.[50] Metz's political theology is at the center of his thinking, articulated in his major work, *Faith in History and Society*. Metz understands politics as humans taking responsibility for shaping history.

Essential to Metz's theology is his daring stance on theodical reflection that reoccurs throughout his thinking. Metz offers an inventively sharp critique of theodicy itself explaining: "The kind of theology I am trying to work out and convey here cannot solve the theodicy question." "Rather," he writes, "it consists in formulating it as a question directed back at God."[51] Thus Metz breaks with his contemporaries such as Jürgen Moltmann, Karl Barth, Peter Koslowski, Eberhard Jüngel, Dietrich Bonhoeffer, and even Catholic theologians Karl Rahner and Hans Urs von Balthasar. Their theodical reasoning begins with the notion of a God of pathos and invokes the incarnation as their response to human suffering; Christ's suffering and death on the cross unites human pain and divine love. In this way God is removed from the position of being a distant spectator and becomes a participant in human pain.[52]

Yet, for Metz, this theological response simply reiterates the traditional theodical attempts to exonerate God, thus easing the theodical tension between divine omnipotence and suffering. Instead, Metz decisively questions: "How is a discourse on the suffering God not just a sublime duplication of human suffering and human powerlessness?"[53] Metz's critique of the God of pathos echoes the criticism of Moltmann as "too speculative,"[54] and the God of pathos portrays God as weak and only as a fellow sufferer. For Metz, Christ's suffering does not resolve human suffering or respond to ever-lingering questions of innocent suffering.

The God of pathos is also contrary to one of Metz's fundamental theological dissatisfactions; the formulation of "fixed" systematic concepts of God. In the end, for Metz, theodical resolutions based on a suffering God are all too neat, too rational, and too pristine a solution. They avoid the reality that suffering itself possesses the potency to change society. And precisely this recollection of suffering served in the construction of Metz's now famous "dangerous memory."[55] Of the classic theodical struggle to "justify" God, Metz advances his own priority for the historical by saying, "If anything, God will 'justify' himself in God's own time in the face of history of suffering."[56]

Metz displays a profound respect for the innately complex nature of both the divine and the human experience of suffering.

Metz views the suffering of Christ as central to the mystery of human suffering, but he challenges Christians to recall Christ's "poverty of spirit." In so doing, Metz seizes the innate power of suffering as a means of understanding and dealing with suffering in a process of Christian theology and praxis. In fact, Metz understands the spiritual enterprise as "to become fully human" as grounded in Christlike spiritual poverty. Metz develops the essential relationship between humanity and poverty, saying that "to become human means to become 'poor,' to have nothing that one might brag about before God. . . . Becoming human involves proclaiming the poverty of human spirit in the face of the total claims of a transcendent God."[57] For Metz, the praxis of poverty of spirit supersedes speculative theodical argumentation.

Thus we arrive at the core of Metz's theology represented in his oft-quoted expression of "dangerous memory." The church is founded on the remembrance of the passion and death of Jesus Christ. For Metz, memory is an attempt to recover the truths that reveal a history of human suffering and to join them to the suffering of Christ. The *danger* of this memory arises from its call for social awareness and the hard-earned change to follow. Thus, memory possesses not only a past but also a present and future orientation. Metz envisions the recollection of those who suffered as an impetus to uncover the causes of their suffering and reconsider them in order to avoid past mistakes and formulate strategies for resisting and eliminating suffering. Memory "badgers the present and calls it into question," Metz writes. "It compels believers to be in a continual state of transformation in order to take this future into account."[58] Learning from the past means memory can liberate; recalling the past can prompt persons to an awareness of collective suffering. Recollection of past suffering also points to the reign of God to come, a time when God will redeem all those who suffered in the past.[59]

So Metz argues for "dangerous memory." Theodical thinking silences the potency of the memory of those who have suffered

with argumentative soteriology that uncritically and falsely rec-
onciles. "[With] the suffering God," he asks, "does not something
like a secret aestheticization of all suffering secretly come into
play?"[60] The consequence of such "aestheticization," Metz believes, is a middle-class apathy that breeds hopelessness, because
no efforts are made to avoid future unnecessary suffering. Metz
insists that the middle class must face human suffering; otherwise
it will be content with its indulgent lifestyle and lack the impetus
to protest against suffering.

For Metz, memory is exemplified in narratives. Metz prioritizes narratives from the Hebrew scriptures such as Exodus, the
stories of the prophets, and Job, because they provide examples
he understands as "mystical" processes of responding with faith
and hope to suffering that cannot be transcended. Metz points out
that Job's suffering is not relieved but rather engaged in a process
of deeper self-surrender—"a poverty of spirit." In the Christian
Gospels Metz finds Jesus' example of resounding poverty to be
"the poverty of misery and neediness. Jesus was no stranger to this
poverty either. He was a beggar, knocking on people's doors. He
knew hunger, exile and the loneliness of the outcast. . . . He had no
place to lay his head, not even in death—except a gibbet on which
to stretch his body."[61] Furthermore, Jesus demonstrated continual
concern for the poor, weak, oppressed, and marginalized. The in-
justices these lowly ones endured relate to Metz's future-oriented
eschatological vision, where the poor of spirit will be justified in
the reign of God. The resurrection is also integral to the "dangerous memory," because at its core, it represents this same triumph
over injustice and suffering, with hope in the future reign of God.
Yet it is essential to note that Metz definitively dismisses a notion
of the resurrection without its prior suffering of the crucifixion.
By giving priority to narrative theology over argumentative theology, Metz illustrates the importance he places on making sense of
such religious experience as human suffering, which is difficult to
capture with abstract doctrinal theologizing.[62]

Metz advances an alternative theology, referred to as theodicy-sensitive. In Metz's theological framework, faith and suffering are not in disaccord. On the contrary, faith is precisely the appropriate response to suffering because it avoids theodical argumentation in the hope of resolve. Metz points to prophetic examples of faith (Job and Jesus) that can be found in the scriptures, where faith serves as a response to collective suffering rather than an intellectualized response. Thus, Metz is willing to abide with the lingering traditional and hard-pressed theodical questions as well as human anguish itself. Metz arrives at the mystical theology of suffering with a "solidarity of hope" that bonds all Christians—living and dead.

> Solidarity that proves itself not only in relation to the living and coming generations, but also in relation to the dead. With this hope the Christian is not hoping primarily for himself or herself, but rather for the other, and in and through this, for himself and herself. The hope that Christians have in the God of the living and the dead, in God's power to raise the dead, is the hope for a revolution on behalf of everyone, those who suffer unjustly, those long ago forgotten, indeed, even the dead.[63]

According to Pinnock, Metz deeply ponders but retreats from a theologizing resolution to the Holocaust, contending that Christian responses to suffering must give the priority of interpretation to the Holocaust victims, survivors, and the Jews themselves in their theological and personal struggle to make some sense of this catastrophe. Pinnock appropriately summarizes Metz's position, which emerges from his theodical stance: "Metz concurs with Holocaust survivor Elie Wiesel in exposing the lack of answers to the questions that innocent suffering poses, and in rejecting theistic theodicy explanations and justifications as offering neither intellectual nor emotional conformation in the face of Auschwitz."[64] Metz boldly holds that the suffering at Auschwitz remains silent to any theological justification. In fact, unlike many other Christian theologians who identify the Holocaust victims with the suffering of Christ, Metz takes the dissimilar stand that Jesus' suffering does not compare with such human suffering. Jesus freely chose his suffering, unlike the horrible and senseless suffering of, for example, the more than one million children who were murdered in the Holocaust. Therefore, for Metz, the human suffering of the Holocaust is even more scandalous than divine suffering.

A GOD OF PATHOS AND THE JUÁREZ-CHIHUAHUA FEMINICIDES?

After reviewing these three post-Shoah theologies of suffering, I return to the question of God's relationship with the Juárez feminicides and senseless suffering. I contend that within the boundaries of traditional theodical reasoning we can say that God unquestionably offers more than a distant sympathy for human suffering. God establishes solidarity with, is on the side of, and is present with the suffering women and their survivors. God's solidarity with the *godless* and *godforsaken* of Juárez, as Moltmann would put it, is an appropriate description of the anguish of the dead women and their families and communities.

Consideration of these women's deaths devoid of God's solidarity definitively changes the entire landscape of our understanding of what is occurring in Northern Mexico. Without God's presence in the midst of this horror, our understanding of the mayhem and thus our responses to it could only be despair or atheism. Belief in God's solidarity with these suffering women not only challenges our faith but also demands action. Yet it is precisely the nature of this solidarity with the suffering women that remains one of the most salient contemporary theological challenges of our time. It is a tempting leap to an understanding of the God of pathos; however, a God who is intimately suffering with these women, as Metz shows, raises almost as many issues as it resolves. A God of pathos does not resolve the key theological question of the Juárez-Chihuahua feminicides, which is the question of senseless suffering. Such a leap also compromises God's omnipotence in favor of God's omni-benevolence.

I return to Metz, whom I see as offering an alternative to traditional theodical methodology with its irreconcilable opposition between the divine "omni" attributes and human suffering. One of Metz's outstanding contributions is a methodological shift from traditional theodical inquiry. He points to other means and perspectives in dealing with the age-old question of the relationship of God and human pain. Interestingly, Soelle and Metz also propose that faith and a solidarity of hope transcend the traditional theodical argumentation. Soelle, for example, points to an acceptance that supersedes the theodical question.[65] I consider these responses to suffering in the next chapter.

I add one essential comment, returning to the Book of Job and employing Gustavo Gutiérrez's interpretation and theological reflection on chapter 9 of Job as critical in understanding the entire work. At this point in the narration, Job cries out with a paroxysm of suffering that demands justice from God while simultaneously appealing for a divine arbiter. In utter desperation, Job pleads with the renowned verse, "I know: my Avenger [G_'_l] lives" (Job 19:25). (A more familiar translation of this verse is, "I know that my Redeemer lives."[66]) In this verse Job calls God "go'el," which signifies both a defender and avenger. For Job, the God who inflicted his suffering is the same God in whom Job has placed his hope of mercy. (We have seen Soelle take issue with this dualist logic in her critique of Moltmann; now we see Gutiérrez employ the same logic and arrive at a sobering insight.)

Let's take a close look at the word *go'el*. The term emerges from the experience of the ancient Hebrew familial law where it was the duty of a near relative to protect or defend the rights of another family member when need be.[67] The Hebrews applied this term to the Divine. Such usage defines their covenant relationship as one grounded in the likeness of a familial bond of solidarity. God is a family member who both protects and defends. Or in Gutiérrez's words, "the word go'el came out of the Jewish people's experience of solidarity." And like the nearest relative, God takes responsibility for "His people." Yet this rapport comes with the complexity of a God, who seems to act in a divided manner. God both inflicts and avenges the Hebrew people. Gutiérrez comments, "Job, as it were, splits God in two and produces a God who is judge and a God who will defend him at that supreme moment; a God whom he experiences as almost an enemy but whom he knows at the same time to be truly a friend. . . . These are two sides of the one God."[68]

What are we to make of such duality? The usage of *go'el* in the Book of Job is a theodical problem turned on its ear. The duality expressed in *go'el* responds to the irreconcilable problem of conflicting divine attributes. How can God be both inflictor (omnipotent/omniscient) of suffering and redeemer (omnibenevolent) from suffering? Instead of attempting to reconcile these attributes, Job divides God, conceiving a sort of "schizoid Divinity" where these two attributes coexist, though clearly Job places unfailing trust in the high road of God's benevolence. Yet we are left with a puzzling question: Can Divinity protect against Divinity? Rather than stumble on Job's "painful, dialectical" usage of *go'el,* Gutiérrez seizes what he sees in this terminology as "one of the most profound messages" of the work of Job. This confounding logic of *go'el* suggests that "any approach to the mystery of God must be complex,"[69] says Gutiérrez. He points beyond the argumentative nature and dualistic conflict to the theodical problem itself, to gaze with a profound appreciation of the theological process as well as the Divine. As Gutiérrez insists, approaching the mystery of God is not a simple but a complex matter.[70] He reminds us that to ponder the nature of God is to enter into the realm of ineffable mystery. Surely, we humbly keep this "mystery" as an indispensable factor in the forefront of our consideration of any human anguish, whether the feminicides in Juárez or our own anguish.

CONCLUSION

Some human suffering can yield good fruit. Suffering, for example, may help us learn from and avoid past mistakes. Suffering may spark the fervor of hope and courage to get us through a life crisis. Suffering can mute selfishness and awaken in us a new-found and nobler self, making us better, stronger, and more appreciative and loving. This is particularly true in the case of moral suffering, where people willingly take on pain in a purposeful challenge to oppressive structures that impose human misery. Yet just when we think we have some understanding of suffering, we are confronted with senseless suffering—naked anguish seemingly without redemptive meaning. None of us is impervious to the senseless suffering of illness, death, accident, or random or targeted violence. Our hard-learned responses to managing suffering in our lives, along with the meanings that make suffering in some ways understandable, or at least bearable, can evaporate in an instant. Senseless suffering reminds us that all suffering is an ineffable mystery, a nebulous territory where we acquiesce to mystery, fall into despair, or rebel with atheistic rage.

The appalling gallows murder of an innocent child in Wiesel's narrative represents a single instance of the almost inconceivable genocide of six million Jews. The Juárez-Chihuahua feminicides in Northern Mexico exemplify senseless suffering: the women are innocent; their deaths occur seemingly devoid of redemptive meaning. Always compounding this senselessness are the causes of this suffering. Natural or accidental suffering is troubling enough, but when humans inflict cruelty and brutality, it escalates the senseless into dystopia. In Juárez, we see this immediate insanity of perpetrators play out, but we also observe an oppressive social, economic, and political environment that imposes conditions that create senseless suffering.

The senseless suffering of World War II triggered Moltmann, Soelle, and Metz to search their respective religious traditions for comprehensive responses, which they found wanting. Consequently, each theologian devoted his or her life to relentless questioning. Surely Moltmann's attempt to humanize divine disposition and solidarity with the suffering of the world captures the spirit of the mid-twentieth-century rethinking of the theodical problem that distances itself from a pure theistic notion of God. He strives to resolve the seeming abyss between human anguish and the Divine by conceiving a complex dynamic of inner-trinitarian suffering. His resolution to the theodical rub is to bond human and divine suffering to this trinitarian suffering. Thus, he preserves divine integrity with a God of pathos, a God who knows and feels pain in a manner that is distinct from, but bonded with, human suffering. With regard to the Juárez-Chihuahua feminicides, Moltmann's theological construct is founded on a complex Father-Son dynamic that remains blatantly and exclusive androcentric. This might seem disconcerting and it certainly is when applied to the suffering of the women of Juárez, who are victims of patriarchal societal norms and were killed at the hands of men.

Soelle, while following Moltmann's path, does not decisively craft a systematic discourse on the nature of this divine presence but employs what she refers to as "particular" instances of human pain to illuminate her stance of an all-loving God present in human affliction. In *Suffering*, Soelle prioritizes narratives as potent theological resources, grounding her theology in moving examples of human pain rather than theorized discourse. One of

Soelle's theodical tacks is to compromise divine omnipotence in favor of divine compassion. But as with Moltmann this admirable, understandable, and enormously appealing posture of a God of pathos raises at least as many issues than it resolves.

Metz's theology of "dangerous memory" avoids abstract theodical argumentation in favor of the acceptance of suffering in a sublime theology of "poverty of spirit" that challenges the conversion of the middle class. In this way Metz, though distancing himself from traditional theodical reasoning, has also preserved the divine attributes of omnipotence, omnipresence, and omnibenevolence. Like Soelle, Metz theologizes down the path of practical application rather than conceptual discourse, prioritizing narratives as a theological method. Metz's theology is not without its critics. Pinnock targets Metz's "dangerous memory," saying, "the role of dangerous memory remains entrapped in bourgeois assumptions." Therefore, we must ask: What is the real role of memory for the actual victims of trauma? "From a victim's position, the memory of suffering may merely reproduce the painful symptom of trauma and bear destructive psychological consequences," Pinnock says. "In extreme cases . . . memory may reinforce hopelessness and motivate passive acceptance, rather than empowering struggle against the weight of suffering."[71] Thus dangerous memory in psychological and spiritual terms remains underdeveloped from the position of the victim.

Most important is that these theologians share a common voice with regard to responses to suffering, particularly senseless suffering, which remains at the crux of the theodical inquiry. They collectively dismiss the former understanding of unconditional acceptance understood as the will of God and instead advance a more humane and practical response of questioning, protest, and lament. Each theologian cites the biblical traditions of the psalms, the prophets, Job, and Jesus himself as examples of responses to pain voiced to God the Father. Thus far, I have considered only the core of these theologians' work, yet each of these theologians in the development of his or her work eventually ascends to a more mystical understanding of divine love and human pain, as does his or her response to suffering. The next chapter takes up the task of presenting some of these responses.

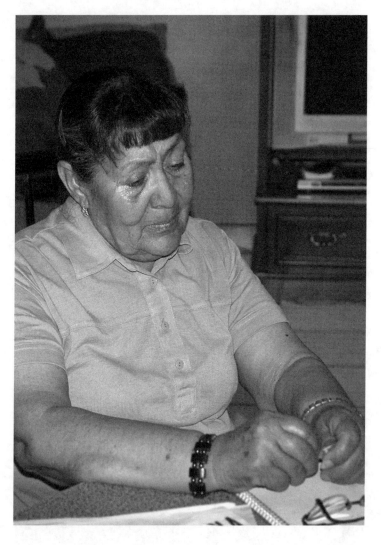

Draining the pain through poetry. *Evangelina Arce has searched for her daughter Silvia for thirteen years, since her disappearance on March 11, 1998. Since authorities have not been able to give her an answer, she has opted to write poetry to lament her pain.*

7

Responses to Suffering

*Who will separate us from the love of
Christ? . . . For I am certain that neither death nor life, neither angels nor
principalities, neither the present nor
the future, nor powers, neither height
nor depth nor any other creature, will be
able to separate us from the love of God.*

—Romans 8:35a, 38–39

ESTHER CHÁVEZ CANO

Esther Chávez Cano was born June 2, 1933, in the city of
Chihuahua. Her father's premature death and her mother's
debilitating depression made virtual orphans of Chávez and her
seven brothers and two sisters.[1] Chávez moved to Juárez in the
1980s. Friends describe her as diminutive, soft-spoken, and hos-
pitable. She never married. Chávez had a love-hate relationship
with her adopted city and its residents. "As a border city, we're
sandwiched in between the terrible U.S. demand for anything
illegal and Mexican greed and corruption," she once lamented.
"Poor Juárez."[2]

Long before most cared, Chávez kept track of the slain women
in Juárez. She collected newspaper clippings as well as detailed
information recounting "how the victim was killed, how the body

was discovered, the name of the person who found her, and the way in which news of the death was made public."[3] Such documentation became invaluable in an environment where government and law officials were manipulating, destroying, or simply failing to compile evidence of the feminicides. Chávez provided copies of her materials to anyone who asked.[4] In November 2007 she donated her papers to the New Mexico State University library. NMSU's executive vice-president and provost Dr. Waded Cruzado-Salas praised Esther's work for ensuring that "the voices of the silenced" will not be forgotten.[5] Such methodical documentation was not surprising from a woman who worked as a corporate accountant for U.S. manufacturers in Mexico, including Kraft Foods. Her retirement in 1992 proved to be timely, as the first corpse was discovered in 1993.

Another of Esther's contributions was the February 1999 founding of the nonprofit Casa Amiga, an old house in Juárez that was converted to serve as a refuge of "survival and healing for violence-tormented women and children."[6] For years, Casa Amiga was the only facility of its kind in Northern Mexico. The once-struggling center eventually garnered support from various organizations, however, and the refuge today occupies a large, modern facility and serves thousands of clients each year. In 2007 Esther's concern for the needs of abused women in Juárez led her to open another house in the original downtown location. "I don't know if I have time, but it's urgent for me to open another [Casa Amiga]," she said in November that year.[7] When asked what originally prompted her to start Casa Amiga, she responded, "Because I am a woman, because I felt helpless, and because I have a conscience."[8]

Countless battles with the Chihuahua state and municipal governments forged Chávez into a seasoned activist with international influence. She denounced what she perceived to be indifference toward violence against women in Juárez. "Women are occupying the space of men in a culture of absolute dominance of men over women," Chávez explained.[9] She is often credited with bringing the feminicides to the attention of the international community. She hounded government officials and embarrassed politicians until they established a special prosecutorial division for female deaths and sexual crimes. This triumph was followed by others, including a new domestic-violence law, systemic legal reforms, and the attention of national and international human rights organizations being brought to bear on women's struggles in Juárez.[10]

Chávez often spoke of a "lack of political will" to investigate and stop the feminicides, along with a "cover-up" that translated into scores of perpetrators going unpunished.[11] "They pretend these are not serial crimes," she said. "It just brings out your rage. It makes you boil."[12] She blasted President Felipe Calderón when he named Arturo Chávez-Chávez as Mexico's attorney general, since he had served as the state prosecutor overseeing Ciudad Juárez during the woman-killings.[13] "Any investigation should start with the police force," she suggested.[14] "There's a cop or an ex-cop involved in many of the Juárez crimes. It's known that there's a pact between the police and those who sell drugs."[15]

As her reputation grew, so did accusations that she was pocketing funds and that her efforts were self-aggrandizing. At first Chávez was shocked by such claims, but she later dismissed them as a government ploy to shift the focus of attention from the real issues facing women on the border.[16] "The police hate her, [but they] don't ignore her," said poet Bobby Byrd, a friend of Chávez. "If anything, the authorities wanted to keep activists like Esther quiet because she brought attention to the vacuum of justice in Juárez."[17]

A 2003 picture seems to capture the essence of Chávez. Amid a crowd of protestors toting the emblematic pink crosses, Chávez stands defiantly, arms crossed, her gray hair falling loosely about her head, a determined scowl on her face. Photographs of Chávez never capture her smiling, as if she were perpetually unsatisfied, as if her thoughts were always on the work remaining to be done.[18]

Chávez received numerous awards for her work, including Mexico's National Human Rights Award in 2008. Also in 2008 the Inter-American Court of Human Rights ruled that Mexico violated human rights conventions by failing to investigate adequately the 2001 murders of three women in Juárez.[19] Chávez once said that hearing "the voice of the woman . . . requires twice the energy, twice the intensity of a man's voice. . . . This is why I learned to shout for those who couldn't . . . and to cry so many times for and with so many women, girls and boys whose voices and whose lives have been crushed by the impunity of our state and nation."[20] Sadly for those fighting to end the Juárez woman-killings, Esther died Christmas Day 2009.

This chapter considers responses to human suffering. First, we examine the response of those immediately plagued with affliction: the survivors. These are various overlapping and progressive stages of healing. The initial shock of a "great pain" that renders one mute is followed by questioning, protest, solidarity, and finally acceptance. In the second portion of this chapter I pose an ethical challenge to those of us who learn of these killings.

FROM MUTE SUFFERING TO ACCEPTANCE

It is difficult to imagine the shock of family members, such as Paula Bonilla-Flores, who had to identify the mutilated remains of her daughter, Sagrario. Simone Weil and Dorothee Soelle contend that genuine affliction renders a person numb and mute. This silent suffering has broad and long-lasting consequences that can prove devastating. Preoccupation with suffering isolates mute sufferers from themselves, others, and the outside world. For example, they may not be able to care for themselves or those they love; they may even be unable to accept the care that loved ones or even professional caretakers extend. Of this silent state of human stagnation Soelle writes, "The weight of unbearable suffering makes us feel totally helpless; we are stripped of the autonomy to think, speak, or act."[21] On a long-term basis, unless the person finds a way to express his or her pain, suicide becomes a real option because the person has lost all sensation. Pent-up pain makes any potentially liberating discourse impossible, thus blocking the healing process.

On various occasions in the Gospels, Jesus expresses compassion for mute sufferers. In Mark's Gospel such a healing occasion occurs for a deaf man with a speech impediment. "Some people" bring the man to Jesus, suggesting that he was unable to approach Jesus on his own. They "begged him to lay his hands on him" (Mk 7:33). Jesus begins by taking the man away from the crowd so the two are alone. This confrontation with mute suffering is appropriately characterized not with words but by compassionate, tactile expressions. Jesus puts his fingers into the man's ears and then uses his own spittle to touch the man's tongue. Only then is the silence broken, though still not with words. The Gospel refers to Jesus emitting a "groan," an ache that comes from the very depth of Jesus' spirit. Finally Jesus speaks: "*Ephphatha*—that is 'be open.'" "At once the man's ears are opened; he is freed from the impediment and begins to speak plainly" (Mk 7:35). At this point, the healed man oddly fades from the narrative, and the distant crowd reenters and takes center stage. The crowd proclaims what has happened, though Jesus orders them to stop. "Their amazement went beyond all bounds," Mark says (7:37). In opposition to the once-silent mute suffering of the man, the miracle story closes with the crowd zealously proclaiming the good news: "He makes the deaf hear and the mute speak!" (7:37). The liberation of a mute sufferer facilitates the proclamation of the kingdom that is present and yet to come.[22]

Lament

The first constructive response to overcoming suffering is to excise numb and mute spirits by giving voice to their suffering with language. These are the cries of lament, the language of making sense of suffering not by logic but often by the process of affective expression. People must discover for themselves a way to identify and express their pain; it is not sufficient to have someone speak on their behalf.[23]

Lament initiates a fundamental shift from isolation to communication. This is an all-important step toward establishing solidarity with others, no matter how feeble the first step may be. Such laments counter what can be the overwhelming meaningless, alienation, and powerlessness over suffering. To lament is to take a step to become human again.

Lament is a language of the psalms; in fact, the largest category of the psalter includes forty individual laments and at least twelve national or communal laments.[24] These elegant but no less human prayers address God in a blend of poetry that expresses the anguish of the Hebrew people. The psalms of lament, like the erratic human emotions of muteness from which they rise, are characterized by abrupt shifts. Yet these variations include general components beginning with an invocation of divine assistance followed by descriptions of pressing dire needs, petitions for help and deliverance, vows of praise and sacrifice, and expressions of grateful praise to God.[25] The psalms of lament transcend time and culture, especially when embodying the individual expressions of what sufferers might not dare to articulate on their own: rage, despair, questioning, helplessness, and a type of promissory negotiation with God in return for divine assistance. For our interest here, the psalms' invocation to God marks the first movement, and a prayerful one, from purely reactive muteness to articulation and thus healing. The psalms of lament employed in the liturgy, most often set to music, can capture the pain of a local community or an entire church appealing to God in time of distress. Consider, for example, the enduring Psalm 77, which expresses the lament of those in distress who trust in God and seek divine consolation:

> Aloud to God I cry;
> Aloud to God, to hear me;
> on the day of distress I seek the Lord.
> By night and hands are stretched out with flag-
>   ging;
> My soul refuses comfort.
> When I remember God, I moan;
> when I ponder, my spirit grows faint.
>   (Ps 77:1–4, SJNAB)

A vivid example of the lament process occurred the evening I met with survivors in the group Comité de Madres de Jóvenes Desaparecides—Mother's Committee of Missing Young Women.[26] We gathered on June 15, 2011, at one of the survivor's homes. With hundreds of pictures of missing women laid on the kitchen table before us, I listened to four mothers, one father, and a number of siblings lament long into the night. They told stories not only of their missing daughters and sisters but also of the outrage they felt at the injustice of the corrupt Mexican social, economic, and political systems that they felt had left them no recourse. The group gathered not only to recall the memory of their daughters and sisters but also to seek justice for their murders. I observed something remarkable in this meeting. The committee served as a circle of lament, a place where members found mutual understanding. Moreover, even though these humble people never imagined themselves as activists, solidarity arose from their shared lament, and it was followed by active protest.

I will never forget one mother, Evangelina Arce, whose daughter Silvia disappeared on March 11, 1998, thirteen years prior to our meeting. Evangelina was one of the first women to protest the feminicides publicly. Even after so many years, she still shed rivers of tears when describing Silvia and has continued to search daily for her daughter. That evening at the gathering Evangelina brought a notebook filled with poetry that she read aloud to us. I heard in her words not only anguished grief but also rousing prophetic protests. Her psalms of lament told of Juárez's lost daughters and were an outcry against the city's madness. Clearly, Evangelina's lament assisted her and the others in the group to grapple with the meaning of their lost daughters. Two selections from Evangelina's many writings reveal a powerful means for struggling with the powerlessness and alienation that attend the senseless suffering of their missing and deceased daughters and sisters:

> She was my only daughter. . . .
> Only ice remains in my empty heart, nothing
>   more exists
> The loneliness of this city
> I smell her scent in her clothing; the emptiness
>   of her clothing
> My life destroyed!

> God, with your power and mercy you give us
>   each moment to think,
>   to recuperate from exhaustion and weakness,
> so that we can continue forward and demand
>   justice
> even though the years have passed we must have
>   faith and hope,
> and be prepared to continue fighting. . . .
> Jesus, you care and bless us. Give us strength.
> I am hopeful that I find my daughter alive![27]

Question and Protest

Questioning is one of the initial and ongoing responses to tragedy that fuels theodical reflection. Questioning the senseless suffering of the murdered women is the impetus for this work. Jürgen Moltmann, Dorothee Soelle, and Johann Baptist Metz show that protesting against suffering is an age-old response found in prophetic biblical figures such as Job and the prophets and amid the psalms of lament. The definitive moment for Christians, as Moltmann so well describes, is Christ's final death cry on the cross: "My God, my God, why have you forsaken me?" (Mk 15:22). While ever faithful to his Father's divine love, Jesus questions the manner of God's righteousness in the world while simultaneously taking up humanity's protest against suffering.[28]

Post-Shoah theological debate engaged in reformulating a theology of suffering and in advancing protest through both prayer and action as valid Christian responses to suffering (as opposed to unconditional surrender). Furthermore, protest must counter historically imposed suffering. Heroic and saintly examples of protesters who fought to eliminate unnecessary suffering capture our imaginations—Martin Luther King, Jr., Cesar Chavez, and, in response to the Juárez feminicides, Esther Chávez Cano. Simple resignation to unnecessary suffering turns the one who suffers into another victim. On the other hand, protest can dignify and empower those who suffer to take responsibility for their lives and those of their loved ones, regardless of the outcome of their efforts.

Solidarity

As we have seen, cries of lament give rise to solidarity. The suffering communicated is a pain shared and that in itself empowers. Such solidarity also dignifies the survivors, whose human integrity—as with the missing and murdered women—has been violated. Solidarity counters the isolation and alienation innate in human pain. Discovering that others are plagued with relentless questioning helps quiet the self-interrogation that suffering naturally fosters.

Moreover, while senseless suffering may never be understood, it can be shared. This sharing counters such senselessness with meaning, naturally recalling, as Metz has articulated, the "dangerous memory" of those who have been lost. From this lament and recollection comes the call to action as both a memorial to the dead and, it is hoped, a catalyst to societal and structural changes that will prevent future catastrophes. In this way such solidarity spawns hope.

Acceptance

A discussion of the acceptance of suffering must begin with a reiteration of the essential distinction between unconditional surrender and acceptance. Unconditional surrender sees suffering as a punishment from God, inflicted as a consequence of past sin; it generally results in a morbid spirituality of self-pity masked as piety. Acceptance does not operate on the presupposition of a God who fails, punishes, or denies. Nor does it allow for a flight from reality. Furthermore, it dismisses blame, victimization, and fatalism.[29] Instead, true acceptance receives reality as it is, without placing conditions and undue expectations upon it.

This acceptance is characterized by the lack of a need to bend or change reality to one's will; rather, one who accepts chooses to engage and even love reality as it presents itself. Acceptance relinquishes possession and/or control over persons and the insurmountable consequences that reality presents. Acceptance "gives up the fight" to achieve one's own agenda or indulge in compulsions. True acceptance is a disposition of poverty, meaning that it requires one to abandon the expectation of controlling what might come in the future. Thus, it is a dying of self and yet a radical affirmation of life. At best, this acceptance comes with a rich appreciation of the gifts of God's offering.

Acceptance begins with healing transformation. In priestly ministry I have repeatedly observed some of the most moving and dramatic examples of genuine acceptance and its transformative power among recovering addicts. Persons suffering from obsessions with alcohol, drugs, or other stimulants are driven by selfishness and pain. Their addiction will eventually lead to self-destruction. Rather than indulge, control, or fight against these excessive ego drives, acceptance of self and reality is the beginning of their recovery. An exquisite petition of acceptance is the recovery community's adoption of Reinhold Niebuhr's now familiar prayer: "God grant me the serenity to accept things I cannot change, the courage to change the things I can, and the wisdom to know the difference."

Acceptance marks an astonishing turn in the theodical question. Questions as to the cause of suffering, I contend, will always occur, but with true acceptance these questions, as well as the anxieties that accompany them, are superseded by an unlimited love of reality and trust in God.[30] As Paul explained, "We know that God makes all things work together for the good of those who have been called" (Rom 8:28). The more one gives one's self up to this acceptance, the more it is augmented. Soelle made the point that once adopted, acceptance increases with daily practice: "The more strongly we affirm reality, the more we are immersed in it," she noted.[31]

I observed genuine acceptance in Evangelina Arce. I questioned her specifically with regard to holding God accountable for the loss of her daughter. Evangelina's response was surprising. Rather than question God, she instead turned to the Divine for care and strength. Her long suffering and years of searching for her daughter had forged in Evangelina a disposition of acceptance. That said, her acceptance has not hindered her continued search for Silvia and her protests against an unjust system. Seemingly radical dichotomies of lament and protest and solidarity coexist in Evangelina Arce, within the contextual disposition of a profound acceptance of reality.

The Call

The call arrives as grace always does: unexpectedly and with a rush of conflicting reactions. I remember the instant in 1993 when I learned of the feminicides. I was at the breakfast table reading the *Los Angeles Times*. A few lines at the bottom of the page sparingly reported the discovery of five women's bodies discarded in the desert sands of Ciudad Juárez—the first of the hundreds of corpses that, two decades later, continue to be found there. I stopped reading and lifted my head, knowing that something was terribly, terribly wrong. I realize now that in that moment the deaths of these women made their initial claim on me. Not surprisingly, my first emotional reactions (as opposed to theological response) to this call ranged from confusion to disbelief. I found myself caught in the throes of a disturbing internal conflict; my initial desire to turn away from the details of these murders was mixed with an unavoidable compulsion to look. Such a reaction is reminiscent of Rudolf Otto's description of the human reaction to the uniquely religious phenomenon of the *mysterium tremendum et fascinans* (fearful and fascinating mystery).[32] Through the corpses of the women a claim was made on me. I faced the choice of turning away from these dead women, ignoring their beckoning, and going on with my life unbothered, or of responding to their frightening invitation. I know now, despite the many family members, friends, colleagues, and superiors who cautioned me against proceeding, that ignoring this call would have compromised my sense of self. The missing and dead women and their survivors are part of my life now.

THE CALL-RESPONSE DIALECTIC

When viewed solely as a secular phenomenon, the Juárez-Chihuahua feminicides appear to be a meaningless tragedy—a perspective that breeds indifference, despair, and hatred. However, when viewed as a theological event, the murders, though no less horrific, become an occasion of grace, an invitation to engage both the horror of and hope in this theological event. Additionally, through that engagement, we can hear the specific call that God issues to us to take appropriate action to stop these killings.

The *call-response dialectic* occurs between the theological event and each individual who encounters it. The dialectic operates on multiple levels of which I identify three specific moments. The first moment challenges us to *attend actively* to such human suffering as the Juárez-Chihuahua feminicides rather than to respond apathetically. God asks us not to turn away but to stay and find the courage to ponder the kidnapping, rape, murder, and bodily desecration of these young women. This is the call. The challenge to respond to God's call is stark, unyielding, and terrifying. We must weigh this human loss, struggle with the perpetrators' sick aggression, and consider the consequences of structural violence in a society rife with poverty, drug abuse, and corruption. Do we dare take the horror of these victims upon ourselves? Do we force ourselves to look directly at the brutal killings of the women in Northern Mexico? If we answer yes, then we face a new challenge.

In the second moment, we must *make a choice*. On the one hand, we can turn away from the horror of these deaths and choose ignorance, apathy, or despair. This choice may appear the easier, yet it is not without its consequences—the least of which makes us ultimately complicit with the event. On the other hand, we respond to this theological event by becoming participants in the suffering of the dead women and their communities. By so doing, we allow the event and the women themselves to make a claim on us.

But actually engaging these slain women also requires taking concrete action to try to end the tragedy. This is the third moment: the *call to action*. This action may range anywhere from working to change the culture that has enabled the murders to simply helping to make known the plight of the Juárez women. Humanitarians, journalists, artists, academics, and theologians—people from all walks of life in the international community—have responded to the suffering of these women in Juárez.

This call-response dialectic is illustrated in the dilemma presented in the parable of the Good Samaritan (Lk 10:29–37). A traveler on the road from Jerusalem to Jericho falls victim to robbers who strip, beat, and leave him half-dead. Various people—including a priest—pass by and observe the man but only the Samaritan "was moved with compassion at the sight . . . and cared for him" (Lk 10:33b, 35b). In contrast to the other travelers, the Samaritan's disposition to act when he sees the man exemplifies the choice to move from observer to participant when encountering another's suffering. The Samaritan is moved to become part of the man's experience by caring for his wounds and taking him to shelter.

Matthew's renowned description of the Last Judgment contains within it the three moments of the call-response dialectic outlined above. Strictly speaking, this narrative is not a parable but an apocalyptic vision of the reign of God to come, a future time that will justify human suffering. Matthew strategically places this as the last narrative prior to Christ's passion. As the journey of suffering begins for Jesus, the reader is offered this narrative of hope and ultimate justice for the poor and suffering.

At the beginning of the scene the king divides all the nations into two groups. To the group on his right the veil is lifted, and the king discloses his presence in the suffering of humanity. "For I was hungry and you gave me food, I was thirsty and you gave me drink. I was a stranger and you welcomed me, naked and you clothed me. I was ill and you comforted me, in prison and you came to visit me" (Mt 25:36–37).

The second moment of the Last Judgment is the consequence of the decision to either turn away from or to respond to the call. Both those who did and those who did not respond to the needy posed the same query: "Lord, when did we see you hungry, and feed you or see you thirsty and give you drink?" (Mt 25:38). Then a second time, to the group on his left, the king lifts the veil to disclose his presence in the suffering of humanity. "I assure you, as often as you did for one of my least brothers, you did it for me" (Mt 25:41). Those who did not respond maintain that they never saw the king among the needy. "Lord, when did we see you hungry or thirsty or away from home or naked or ill or in prison and not attend you in your needs?" (Mt 25:45). Their rationale of self-exoneration was that the king's presence was concealed among them, implying that had they known the king was in need, they would have taken action to assist him. They maintain their ignorance and deny any apathy, but this rationalization does not pass muster with the king. "Out of my sight, you condemned, into that everlasting fire prepared for the devil and his angels!" he says (Mt 25:41). Those who responded to the suffering are welcomed to eternal life: "Come. You have my Father's blessing! Inherit the kingdom prepared for you from the creation of the world" (Mt 25:35).

This leads to the third moment of the call-response dialectic: the uncompromising nature of the call. Although it is an invitation, there is no middle ground. Salvation or damnation is determined according to the positive or negative response to the call. One must choose a path; there is no neutrality.

THE CONSEQUENCES OF MORAL SUFFERING

The call comes with consequences that can best be understood within the context of *moral suffering*. Moral suffering results from a decision to oppose unjust suffering (referred to in the typology of suffering as "historically imposed suffering"), to take on the burden of another, as the Good Samaritan chose to participate in the suffering of the victimized stranger he encountered. Moral suffering comes as a consequence of protest, resistance, acts of compassion, and any opposition to circumstances under which people are forced to suffer, whatever the nature or cause.

Moral suffering does not come without consequences. To understand these consequences, let us first recall that all suffering is either meaningful (in the sense that we learn from it) or meaningless (in the sense that we do not). What can we learn from moral suffering? First, moral suffering instructs the individual about the breadth and depth of his or her human capacity. It is a lesson in the growth of one's humanity. Esther Chávez knew, from a lifetime of experience, the liability of being a woman living in a society rampant with patriarchy and misogyny. She articulated the helplessness of women subject to systemic marginalization and injustice. Chávez fought to redress this injustice and violence toward women in the border area. But despite her initial doubts about her ability to bring about change, Chávez learned that she possessed the ability to make strides toward the abolition of women's suffering in Juárez.

Moral suffering can also teach us that our opposition to historically imposed suffering comes at a cost. Chávez's positive response to the call meant that she would participate in the suffering of the slain women, and so she experienced various manifestations of moral suffering, including being accused of having self-serving motives and even of embezzling funds. Chávez aroused treacherous, powerful, and violent enemies in Juárez, and she was certainly aware that her work could cost her her life.

But part of moral suffering is the knowledge that we can be an agent to stop suffering. In November 2007, cognizant of her approaching death from cancer, Chávez's primary concern was opening another center for women. Her seventeen-year journey from private citizen to internationally renowned activist had taught her that responding to the call does make a difference.

Coming to understand that our actions bring results is a necessary lesson, because when confronted with suffering on the scale of the Juárez-Chihuahua feminicides, most of us tend to believe that we are incapable of effecting the same level of change as a social reformer such as Chávez. But the real reason for our resistance to action is our unwillingness to pay the cost of opposing historically imposed suffering. Once we understand that we can ameliorate suffering from whatever position we occupy in life, inevitably our understanding of ourselves and of our obligation to our fellow humans must change.

CONCLUSION

The theodical question is never resolved or erased. To a greater or lesser degree we must all engage in a lifelong process of transformation where suffering moves us from the deadness of muteness to hard-earned and, hopefully, loving acceptance of reality as it presents itself. Jesus' death cry articulates the radical questioning of and protest against all suffering; it becomes the raw collective lament uttered not just by Jesus but by all humankind who share this suffering. Jesus' words are also a most appropriate response to the butchering of women at the border.

When considering the Juárez-Chihuahua feminicides, one must stand at the crossroads of a crucial decision: choose despair and hate and be overwhelmed by the crushing and toxic forces of globalization, poverty, corruption, and drug trafficking, or choose hope. This hope groans in lament, nurtures hard questions, voices radical protest, and at best, bonds us in solidarity with others who are afflicted. I observed the afflicted survivors of the missing and dead women, as St. Paul would say, "made strong" through hope manifested in solidarity (2 Cor 12:9–10). For those who willingly choose to engage the Juárez-Chihuahua feminicides, our own world view—and very identity—is subject to transformation, because we have accepted God's invitation to enter into solidarity with the afflicted, the godless, and the godforsaken among us. In so doing we also enter into a greater solidarity with God, who suffers in solidarity. Thus does hope, rather than despair, become the last word on these tragic events.

Epilogue

It is June 15, 2011. The pink crosses are long gone from the intersection of the Ejército National and Paseo de la Victoria, taken down in 2007 by authorities who want this matter forgotten. Yet this ground will always be hallowed by the blood of the bodies discarded here in November 2001 under cover of darkness. I blessed this ground on my first visit to Juárez in 2005. I believe that all of the missing and dead women sanctify this field, which has become a gathering place for remembrance and protest.

A hundred yards to my right, near the busy intersection, some devoted survivors of the victims have tried to erect replacement crosses. Sadly, these makeshift pink planks lay about like the dead women themselves once did, scattered pieces in the dirt.

I kneel, my head bowed. Beyond the city traffic and amid the dusty desert wind, I wait for the dead women to whisper to me. Perhaps they will tell me what I should do next to advance their cause. Perhaps they will reveal to me the clandestine meaning of their suffering, show me an angle from which I can make sense of the madness, a message I can offer to their survivors, people smoldering with affliction, people who cannot stop asking why.

As my back burns from the penetrating Juárez heat, my lips instinctively form the words I always recall when holding the hands of those departing from this world:

> The Lord is my shepherd; I shall not want.
> In verdant pasture he gives me repose;
> Besides restful waters he leads me. . . .
> Even though I walk in the dark valley

> I fear no evil; for you are at my side
> With your rod and staff
> that give me courage. (Ps 23:1–3a, 4)

Whether the representation of the good shepherd is the traditional image of Christ holding a lamb or an anonymous Maryknoll priest recovering the befouled corpse of a child, it is the Lord who accompanies all the godless and godforsaken of the world. It was the Lord who is in solidarity with the *desaparecidas* and feminicides in their unthinkable valley of darkness.

For many, the dark valley of senseless suffering is the border valley of El Paso and Juárez. "The darkness" also suggests the ineffable mystery of suffering, a mystery that forever causes us to question life, a life that never answers this question.[1] This claim of "mystery," then, is not a return to the traditional defensive logic of the theodical question, which attempts to preserve the integrity of the Divine when faced with human misery. Neither is it employed as a last-resort explanation, a catch-all contrivance, a last-chance escape hatch when all logic has failed. It is no *deus ex machina* that avoids meaninglessness and despair by virtue of its seemingly divine origin. Mystery is the nature of suffering. To engage suffering genuinely is to live with this mystery. At whatever practical responses to suffering at which we arrive, they must be regarded in our theological reflections within the context of mystery. Otherwise we may feel our very efforts to respond are in vain, and we may then forget that the mystery inherent in suffering is a call to faith.

I lift my head. In the distance I see the arrival of the protesters I am meeting—family members of victims. They move slowly to the crossing and then, doing their best in the hot sun and desert wind, begin to erect the fallen crosses. A single cross stands, then another, now two more. Soon all of the fallen crosses will be made upright. I rise and go to assist them.

Notes

Preface

1. See, for example, Charles Bowden, *Juárez: The Laboratory of Our Future*, photographs by Jaime Bailleres (New York: Aperture, 1998).

2. I have found the following works more helpful than any instruction or manual on photography: Roland Barthes, *Camera Lucida: Reflections on Photography*, trans. Richard Howard (New York: Hill and Wang, 2010); Barthes, *A Barthes Reader*, ed. and intro. Susan Sontag (New York: Hill and Wang, 1982); and Susan Sontag, *On Photography* (New York: Picador, 1977). See also Saul Bellows's essay "Graven Images," *The Best American Essays of the Century*, ed. Joyce Carol Oates and Robert Atawan (New York: Houghton Mifflin, 2000), 564–68.

Introduction: What Remains?

1. Mexican authorities removed the crosses in February 2007.

2. For a detailed listing of these victims, see Diana Washington Valdez, *The Killing Fields: Harvest of Women* (Burbank, CA: Peace at the Border, 2006), 301.

3. The correct legal term in Mexico is *no identificadas*.

4. For example, one male corpse was found with the following words written on his bloody t-shirt: "To those who don't believe it and don't have loyalty, greetings." See William Finnegan, "Silver or Lead," *New Yorker* (May 31, 2010), 39–50.

5. Reports estimating the number of murdered and missing women vary greatly. Diana Washington Valdez estimates that between 1993 and 2005 approximately 470 girls and women died violently in Juárez (Valdez, *Harvest of Women*, esp. 359–73). Press reports generally estimate the number of murder victims to be four hundred. The exact number of missing women probably will never be determined, but

estimates vary from 250 to 450. According to information provided by the state authorities to the Inter-American Commission on Human Rights (IACHR) special rapporteur, of the people reported missing between 1993 and 2002, 257 remain unaccounted for. See also Amnesty International, "Mexico: Intolerable Killings: Ten Years of Abductions and Murder of Women in Ciudad Juárez and Chihuahua: Summary Report and Appeals Cases" (August 10, 2003), Amnesty International report, amnestyusa.org website.

6. For a case study of the targeted sexual violence against Sagrario Gonzáles Flores, see Rafael Luévano, "A Living Call: The Theological Challenge of the Juárez-Chihuahua Feminicides, *Journal of Feminist Studies in Religion* 24, no. 2 (Fall 2008): 67–76.

7. See Kelly McKenzie, "Woman Found Dead in Juarez Hotel," (February 9, 2008), on "Diana Washington Valdez Blog."

8. According to Pastilí Toledo, "The rate for women in El Salvador is the highest in the region: 13.9 per 100,000. In Guatemala, the rate is 9.8 per 100,000 women, and in Mexican states such as Chihuahua, Baja California, and Guerrero, the rate has almost tripled from 2005 to 2009, to 11.1 per 100,000. Conversely, rates in countries such as Chile and Argentina are no more than 1.4 per 100,000. That difference underscores a fundamental reality: violence associated with the 'war on drug trafficking' and organized crime—including state corruption—in some countries has specific consequences for women. Just as in war, cruelly raping women is symbolic: it creates cohesion within armed groups, reaffirms 'masculinity,' and is a form of attacking 'the enemy's morale.' But 'domestic' violence is also worsening: although women all over the world are threatened by their partners, the risk is substantially raised when men have easy access to arms and a very slight probability of being taken to court, as is the case in Mexico and Guatemala, where the rate of impunity is over 95%" (Pastilí Toledo, *Project Syndicate*, News Analysis [August 14, 2011], http://www.project-syndicate.org/commentary/toledo1/English).

9. Tracy Wilkinson, "Esther Chavez Dies at 76: Activist Decried Murders of Women in Ciudad Juárez," *Los Angeles Times*, December 7, 2009, http://www.LATimes.com/news/obituaries/la-me-Esther-Chavez27–2009dec27,0,2288127.story.

10. The newer term actually dates back two centuries and means "one who kills women." The *Oxford English Dictionary*'s entry for *feminicide* includes an example from 1833: "Our transcendent powers of cold-blooded feminicide" (*Compact Oxford English Dictionary* [Oxford: Clarendon Press, 1987], 825).

11. I rely on and quote in part from the following sources to establish the distinctions between *femicide* and *feminicide*: Johanna Ikonen, "Feminicide: The Case in Mexico and Guatemala," Background Paper for the European Parliament, Joint Public Hearing, Brussels (April 19, 2006), http://www.EuroParl.Europa.eu; Guatemala Human Rights Commission/USA; "Fact Sheet," http://www.GHRC-USA.org/Programs/ForWomensRighttoLive/factsheet_feminicide.pdf; Diana E. H. Russell, "Defining Femicide and Related Concepts," in *Femicide in Global Perspectives*, ed. Diana E. H. Russell and Roberta A. Harmes (New York: Teachers College Press, 2001), 12–25. I am also indebted to Nancy Piñeda-Madrid for our conversation on this topic.

12. Many scholars, media organizations, and human rights organizations employ the term *feminicide* so as to liken it to genocide. They specifically draw a parallel between the mid-twentieth-century Jewish Holocaust and the more recent killings in Juárez and Chihuahua. While in no way do I wish to diminish the significance of the atrocities in Northern Mexico, I find the analogy tenuous and exaggerated. The basis for correspondence between feminicide and genocide is the extraordinary body count in Northern Mexico. But consider the disproportionate nature of the death tolls (five hundred in contemporary Mexico compared to six million in World War II Europe). Furthermore, by definition, genocide attempts to extinguish an entire race of people, irrespective of gender, class, or age, whereas feminicide is a targeted, gender-based attack. Moreover, the Juárez-Chihuahua feminicides clearly target a specific type and class of female.

13. For the methodology of this consideration, I am indebted to Dorothee Soelle's critique of suffering, especially *Suffering*, trans. Everett R. Kalin (Philadelphia: Fortress Press, 1975).

14. Cf. ibid., 6.

15. Steven S. Volk and Marian E. Schlotterbeck address a secular understanding of the "social anxiety and what is revealed" by the

Juárez-Chihuahua feminicides by considering various cultural/artistic responses to these murders and disappearances. See "Gender, Order, and Femicide: Reading of Popular Culture of Murder in Ciudad Juárez," *Aztlán: A Journal of Chicano Studies* 32, no. 1 (Spring 2007): 53–86.

16. *Compact Oxford English Dictionary*, 459.

17. Linda Rosa Fregoso, "Voices without Echo: The Global Gendered Apartheid," *Emergences: Journal for the Study of Media and Composite Cultures* 10, no. 1 (2000): 137–55.

18. Ibid. Scholars have grouped and named the causative factors for the feminicides in a number of ways. For example, in *Violence and Activism at the Border: Gender, Fear and Everyday Life in Ciudad Juárez* (Austin: University of Texas Press, 2008), Kathleen Staudt refers to three "conceptual frameworks": (1) the global economy, (2) institutions, and (3) culture. Meanwhile, Melissa W. Wright, in "The Dialectics of Still Life: Murder, Women, and Maquiladora," in *Women and Migration in the U.S. Borderlands,* ed. Denise A. Segura and Patricia Zavella (Durham, NC: Duke University Press, 2007), employs the term "death narratives," though these narratives are not to be confused with Uma Narayan's usage of the phrase *death by culture* in her *Dis-locating Cultures: Identity, Traditions, and Third-World Feminism* (New York: Routledge, 1997).

I. Juárez

1. Charles Bowden, *Juárez: The Laboratory of the Future* (New York: Aperture Foundation, 1998).

2. "'Borderplex' is a term for the Texas and Mexican cities on that border. It is similar to the term 'metroplex' (for Dallas–Fort Worth) from the early 1970s. 'Borderplex' is cited in print from the early 1990s. Laredo, El Paso, and the lower Rio Grande Valley have all called their areas a 'borderplex'" ("The Big Apple" [January 13, 2008], barrypopik.com website.

3. See Lisa Chamberlain, "2 Cities and 4 Bridges Where Commerce Flows," *New York Times* (March 28, 2007).

4. Steven S. Volk and Marian E. Schlotterbeck briefly survey border theory in "Gender, Order, and Femicide: Reading of Popular

Culture of Murder in Ciudad Juárez," *Aztlán: A Journal of Chicano Studies* 32, no. 1 (Spring 2007): 59–86, esp. 55–56.

5. Gloria Anzaldúa, *Borderlands: The New Mestiza—La Frontera* (San Francisco: Spinsters/Aunt Lute, 1997), 3, preface.

6. See Volk and Schlotterbeck, "Gender, Order, and Femicide."

7. See, for example, Radley Balko, "The El Paso Miracle," *Reason. com*, July 6, 2009, reason.com website; and "Inside Mexico's 'Murder Capital,'" Fault Lines, *New American Media* (June 20, 2011), newamericamedia.org website.

8. "Inside Mexico's 'Murder Capital.'"

9. José Luis Sierra, "Poet Meets President, Sicilia Test Calderón on Mexican Drug War," *New American Media* (June 27, 2011), newamericamedia.org website.

10. "Inside Mexico's 'Murder Capital.'"

11. Ibid.

12. Susan Sontag, *On Photography* (New York: Picador, 1977), 20.

13. See, for example, Daniel Lederman, William F. Mahoney, and Luis Servén, *Lessons from NAFTA for Latin American and the Caribbean,* The International Bank for Reconstruction and Development/the World Bank (Palo Alto, CA: Stanford University Press, 2005); Gary Clyde Hufbauer and Jeffrey J. Scott, *NAFTA Revisited* (Washington, DC: Institute for International Economics, 2005); and Sergio Gonzáles Rodrígues, *Huesos en el desierto* (Barcelona: Editorial Anagrama, 2002).

14. For better or worse, the economies of U.S. and Mexican industrialization became enmeshed long before NAFTA. However, my consideration of this shared industrialization begins with the early 1990s, since this directly correlates to the first-known feminicides. For more historical background on this U.S.-Mexican industrialization, see Kathleen Staudt, *Violence and Activism at the Border: Gender, Fear, and Everyday Life in Ciudad Juárez* (Austin: University of Texas Press, 2008), 7ff.

15. Ibid.

16. See "Maquiladoras at a Glance," CorpWatch, www.corpwatch. org website.

17. See Made in Mexico, "What Are Maquiladoras? The Maquiladora Industry," madeinmexicoinc.com website.

18. Under NAFTA, the *maquila* program entitles foreign companies to establish and invest foreign capital in a *maquiladora* in Mexico as well as to manage the company's *maquiladora*. The company is also entitled to special customs treatment—for example, duty-free import of machinery, equipment, parts, and materials, which are considered to be only temporarily located in Mexico. See Aureliano Gonzales Bas, "What Is a Maquiladora?" Manufacturing in Mexico: The Mexican In-Bond (*Maquila*) Program, n.d., http://www.udel.edu/leipzig/texts2/vox128.htm.

19. See Melissa W. Wright, "The Dialectics of Still Life: Murder, Women, and Maquiladoras," in *Women and Migration in the U.S.-Mexico Borderlands*, ed. Denise A. Segura and Patricia Zavella (Durham, NC: Duke University Press, 2007), 191.

20. Staudt, *Violence and Activism at the Border*, 8.

21. I garnered this information from a visit to Johnson Controls in Juárez on April 15, 2005.

22. I learned this during a visit with the parents of feminicide victim Sagrario Hernandez-Hernandez on April 15, 2005.

23. Staudt, *Violence and Activism at the Border*, 45.

24. "Inside Mexico's 'Murder Capital.'"

25. See Chamberlain, "2 Cities and 4 Bridges Where Commerce Flows."

26. See, for example, Staudt, *Violence and Activism at the Border*, 14.

27. See, for example, Francisco Meré, "Rural Migration in Mexico: An Overview," *2007 Agricultural Outlook Forum* (March 1, 2007).

28. Staudt, *Violence and Activism at the Border*, 54.

29. The statistics for population growth come from *Business Frontier*, but these figures predate the implementation of NAFTA and *las invasiones*. Given the nature of these waves of migration, more recent accurate statistics are hard to come by. "Ciudad Juárez population growth exceeded 1.2 million in 2000, up from 800,000 in 1990. The average annual growth over the 10–year period was 5.3 percent. Juárez experienced much higher population growth than the state of Chihuahua and then Mexico as a whole. Chihuahua's average annual population growth during 1990–2000 was 2.5 percent; the corresponding figure for Mexico was 2 percent" (*Business Frontier*, "Economic Update on El Paso del Norte," no. 2 [2001]: 2, dallasfed.org website).

30. Staudt, *Violence and Activism at the Border*, 54.

31. See Alicia Gaspar de Alba, "The Maquiladora Murders, 1993–2003," *Aztlán: A Journal of Chicano Studies* 28, no. 3 (Fall 2003): 1–17, esp. 3; Theresa Rodriguez and Diana Monteé with Lisa Pulitzer, *The Daughter of Juárez* (New York: Atria Books, 2007); and *Hijas de Juárez*, Gallery Event SPARC (October 2002), sparcmurals.org website.

32. Staudt, *Violence and Activism at the Border*, 60. The female participants in this study expressed many personal sentiments, one of which is missing their rural homes.

33. Most Reverend Renato Asenio León, interview by author, March 15, 2005.

34. Robert Almonte, deputy chief of Narcotics Investigations for the El Paso, Texas Police Department, interview by author, March 15, 2005.

35. See Ted Galen Carpenter, "Mexico Is Becoming the Next Colombia," Foreign Policy Briefing, Cato Institute, no. 87 (November 15, 2005), 2, cato.org website.

36. See Staudt, *Violence and Activism at the Border*, 11. For a comprehensive presentation on the narcotrade, see Howard Campbell, *Drug War Zone: Frontline Dispatches from the Streets of El Paso and Juárez* (Austin: University of Texas Press, 2009).

37. See Tony Payan, "The Drug War and the U.S.-Mexico Border: The State of Affairs," *South Atlantic Quarterly* 105, no. 4 (Fall 2006): 863–80, esp. 865.

38. Ibid., 863–65.

39. "President Barack Obama already has called for 1,200 National Guard troops in support roles, along with at least another $500 million in spending on border security" (Suzanne Gamboa, "US-Mexico Border Actually More Fortified Now than 5 Years Ago: AP Spin Meter," *Huffington Post* (June 23, 2010).

40. "A guns-only approach has not stopped drug gangs nor reduced killings, especially in Ciudad Juárez. But Calderón has also said he does not plan to withdraw the nearly 10,000 army troops and federal police officers that have been dispatched to the city" (Tracy Wilkinson, "Calderón Visits Ciudad Juárez," *Los Angeles Times* [February 12, 2010]).

41. See Charles Bowden, *Down by the River* (New York: Simon and Schuster Paperbacks, 2002), 3.

42. Ibid.

43. Tony Payan, quoted in Lise Olsen, "Ciudad Juárez Passes Homicide in 2009, So Far," *Houston Chronicle* (October 21, 2009).

44. Carpenter, "Mexico Is Becoming the New Colombia," 5.

45. Ibid. Carpenter also likens Mexico's drug future to that of Afghanistan.

46. See Payan, "The Drug War," 870.

47. Ibid.

48. Ibid., 872.

49. U.S. Department of Transportation, Research and Innovative Technology Administration, Bureau of Transportation Statistics, Border Crossing/Entry Data; based on data from U.S. Department of Homeland Security, Customs and Border Protection, OMR database, http://www.transtats.bts.gov/BorderCrossing.aspx.

50. Payan, "The Drug War," 870.

51. Phil Jordan, quoted in Staudt, *Violence and Activism at the Border*, 12.

52. Payan, "The Drug War," 867.

53. Secretary Eduardo Romero, quoted in Reyes, "Global Integrity," 3.

54. See Laurie Freeman, "State of Siege: Drug- Related Violence and Corruption in Mexico," WOLA Special Report (June 2006).

55. See Amnesty International, "Mexico: Intolerable Killings: 10 Years of Abductions and Murder of Women in Ciudad Juárez and Chihuahua," amnesty.org website see also UN Committee on the Elimination of Discrimination against Women, "Report on Mexico Produced by the Committee on the Elimination of Discrimination against Women under Article 8 of the Optional Protocol to the Convention, and Relay from Government of Mexico."

56. "Inside Mexico's 'Murder Capital.'"

57. See Matador Network, "What's Going On in . . . Juarez, Mexico," matadorpulse.com website.

58. See Freeman, "State of Siege."

59. See Campbell, *Drug War Zone,* 30–33; and Diana Washington Valdez, "Letter Cites Corruption in Mexico," *El Paso Times* (October 16, 2009).

60. "Inside Mexico's 'Murder Capital.'"

2. What Is Killing the Women?

1. Javier Saucedo Alcalá, "Era una menor la mujer asesinada," *El Diario* [Ciudad Juárez] (March 13, 2006).

2. Kathleen Staudt, *Violence and Activism at the Border: Gender, Fear, and Everyday Life in Ciudad Juárez* (Austin: University of Texas Press, 2008), 8.

3. "The shock expressed by US Critics at the 'modernity' they find in Ciudad Juárez speaks more to their own primitivism than to the contemporary reality of Mexico, where manifestations of 'modern' youth culture have been evident for some time" (Linda Rosa Fregoso, "Voices without Echo: The Global Gendered Apartheid," *Emergences: Journal for the Study of Media and Composite Cultures* 10, no. 1 [2000]: 140). See also Debbie Nathan, "Death Comes to the Maquilas: A Border Story," *The Nation* 264, no. 2 (January 13–20, 2003): 18–22.

4. Melissa W. Wright, "The Dialectics of Still Life: Murder, Women, and Maquiladora," in *Women and Migration in the U.S. Borderlands*, ed. Denise A. Segura and Patricia Zavella (Durham, NC: Duke University Press, 2007), 189.

5. Ibid., 187.

6. Ibid., 188.

7. Ibid.

8. Ibid., 187–88.

9. The *maquiladora* discourse, though specific to Juárez—in particular, to the feminicides—finds its basis in the "death by culture explanation" (Uma Narayan, *Dislocating Cultures: Identities, Traditions, and Third-world Feminism* [New York: Routledge, 1997], 81–117).

10. Wright, "The Dialectics of Still Life," 191.

11. Fregoso notes that "the inference that globalization perpetuates hypersexualization among maquila workers that, in turn leads to their murder (male backlash) tells us very little about the actual women victims of the feminicide. Indeed the analytic framework of this master narrative is based on the inaccurate information: of the over 200 deaths, only 16 of the women were actually *maquila* workers, which is less than 10 percent of the victims. The rest includes a housewife, a secretary, sales clerks, students, domestic, drug dealers, employees

at bars, with a great majority in unknown occupations (but not in the *maquila* industry)" (Fregoso, "Voices without Echo," 143).

12. Wright, "The Dialectics of Still Life," 193, 190.

13. Ibid., 199, 186.

14. Ibid., 186.

15. Ibid., 198.

16. Ibid., 197.

17. Ibid., 186.

18. Nathan, "Death Comes to the Maquilas."

19. Ibid.

20. Staudt, *Violence and Activism at the Border*, 41.

21. For a classic presentation of *machismo,* see Octavio Paz, *The Labyrinth of Solitude and Other Writings* (New York: Grove Press, 1985). See also Staudt's critique of Paz's work in *Violence and Activism at the Border*, 36–37. Also see Matthew C. Gutman, *The Meanings of Macho: Being a Man in Mexico City* (Berkeley and Los Angeles: University of California Press, 2007).

22. Here the term *marianismo* does not refer to the devotional spirituality focused on Mary, the mother of Jesus, though a mythic and historical correlation exists between Stevens's theory and Marian spirituality. See Evelyn P. Stevens, "Marianismo: The Other Face of Machismo in Latin America," in *Female and Male in Latin America*, ed. Ann Pescatello (Pittsburgh: University of Pittsburgh Press, 1973), 82–102.

23. Stevens further explains that "there is near agreement on what a 'real woman' is like and how she should act. Among the characteristics of this ideal are semidivinity, moral superiority and spiritual strength. This spiritual strength engenders abnegation, that is, an infinite capacity for humanity and sacrifice. No self-denial is too great for the Latin American women, no limit can be divined to her vast store of patience, with men of her world. . . . She is also submissive to the demands of the men; husbands, sons, fathers, brothers" (ibid., 94–95). Another characteristic is their sadness. Women act the martyr, their suffering affording them a superiority that is really a disguised means to being loved and admired (Stevens, "Marianismo"). See also Tracy Ehlers, "Debunking Marianismo: Economic Vulnerability and Survival Strategies among Guatemalan Wives," *Ethnology* 30, no. 1 (January 1991): 1–16.

24. As Stevens explains, "Beneath the submissiveness, however, lies the strength of her conviction . . . that men must be humored, for after all, everyone knows that they are *como niños* (like little boys) whose intemperance, foolishness, and obstinacy must be forgiven because 'they can't help the way they are'" (Stevens, "Marianismo," 94).

25. See, for example, Staudt, *Violence and Activism at the Border*, 46.

26. Ibid., 45.

27. Ibid., 46.

28. According to Fregoso, "The patriarchal state's initial preoccupation with women's morality and decency is a form of institutional violence that makes women primarily responsible for the violence directed against them. Thus those women who do not conform to the mother/wife model of womanhood (lesbians, working women, women who express sexual desire, and so forth) are suitably punished. In effect, women are transformed into subjects of surveillance; their decency and morality becomes the object of social control. What's more, shifting the blame towards the victims' moral character in effect naturalizes violence against women" (*Mexican Encounters*, 4–5).

29. Staudt, *Violence and Activism at the Border*, 49.

30. Historically, physical and sexual violence against women has not been criminalized in Mexico, particularly when the perpetrator is an acquaintance or intimate partner. In the mid-nineteenth century legal intervention was possible only if men failed to control unmotivated excessive violence against women whose honor and morality were undisputed. See, for example, Staudt, *Violence and Activism at the Border*, 35.

31. Charles Bowden, "I Wanna Dance with the Strawberry Girl," *Talk* (September 1999), 114.

32. See, for example, Staudt, *Violence and Activism at the Border*, 34.

33. By way of example, Howard Campbell references contemporary folk culture in El Paso and Juárez to demonstrate that the narco-trade is firmly a part of popular/folk culture. Narcotraffickers have replaced La Llorona, El Chamuco, and revolutionary soldiers in the armies of Pancho Villa as the Robin Hood–like figures celebrated in song. Ballads and *narcocorridos* (*rancho* drug songs) capture the imagination of border residents, feeding on Mexicans' culturally innate distrust of government institutions in what is seen as the shared struggle for survival at

the border. See Howard Campbell, "Drug Trafficking Stories: Everyday Forms of Narco-folklore on the U.S.–Mexico Border," *International Journal of Drug Policy* 16 (2005): 326–33.

34. Ibid., 333.

3. What Is Suffering?

1. It is common for residents of the *colonias* never to have learned to drive, since their low incomes often mean they will never own a car.

2. *Pathai* refers to the passions. *Aisthesis* also means "to feel" but signifies physical touch. Pertaining to this discussion is the related English word *apathy*, also derived from this Greek word *pathai*, with a suffix *a* meaning "without." *Apathetic* describes a person without feeling. *The Compact Oxford English Dictionary* (Oxford: Clarendon Press, 1987).

3. I thank my colleague Carmichael Peters for his permission to employ his pertinent reflections on Heidegger's thought. See also Emmanuel Levinas as a useful source for the topic of suffering: Emmanuel Levinas, "Useless Suffering" (1982), in *Entre Nous: Thinking of the Other*, trans. Michael B. Smith and Barbara Harshav (New York: Columbia University Press, 1998).

4. Masao Abe, *Zen and the Modern World: A Third Sequel to Zen and Western Thought*, ed. Steven Heine (Honolulu: University of Hawaii Press, 2003).

5. Simone Weil, *Waiting for God* (New York: Harper Perennial, 1951), 73.

6. Ibid., 68.

7. Ibid., 71.

8. Ibid., 67.

9. Dorothee Soelle, *Suffering* (Philadelphia: Fortress Press, 1975), 13.

10. Weil, *Waiting for God*, 72.

11. Ibid., 68.

12. Gustavo Gutiérrez, *On Job: God-Talk and the Suffering of the Innocent* (Maryknoll, NY: Orbis Books, 2007), 30, 115n13.

13. Robert Ellsberg, "Dorothee Soelle," in *Blessed among All Women: Women, Saints, Prophets, and Witnesses for Our Time* (New York: Crossroad, 2007, 265–67).

14. Seeman offers five different forms of alienation: (1) powerlessness, (2) meaninglessness, (3) normlessness, (4) isolation, and (5) self-estrangement (Melvin Seeman, "On the Meaning of Alienation," *American Sociological Review* 24, no. 6 [December 1959]: 783–91).

15. See Soelle, *Suffering*, 12.

16. Soelle includes only two of the five variant forms of alienation presented by Seeman in "On the Meaning of Alienation."

17. Soelle, *Suffering*, 11.

18. Ibid., 12.

19. The typologies of suffering offered in this chapter are the parlance of suffering that will be employed throughout the rest of this work. As a post-Shoah thinker, Soelle initiates our critical consideration of modern theological understandings of suffering.

20. Kent Paterson, "Femicide Fighter, Esther Chavez Cano, Honored by New Mexico State University," *La Prensa San Diego* (November 21, 2007).

4. What Is God's Relationship to Suffering?

1. Kristiaan Depoortere, *A Different God: A Christian View of Suffering* (Louvain, Belgium: Peeters Press, 1995), 27–48. For another treatment, see Paul Froese and Christopher Bader, *America's Four Gods: What We Say about God—and What That Says about Us* (New York: Oxford University Press, 2010).

2. Depoortere, *A Different God*, 1.

3. Ibid., 28.

4. Cf. Dorothee Soelle, *Suffering* (Philadelphia: Fortress Press, 1973), 21. I am indebted to Kristiaan Depoortere for his presentation of these divine representations.

5. Depoortere, *A Different God*, 28.

6. For a New Testament example of this understanding of divine retribution, see the Man Born Blind (Jn 9:1–41).

7. Depoortere, *A Different God*, 33.

8. Harold S. Kushner, *When Bad Things Happen to Good People* (New York: Quill, 1981), 10–11.

9. Depoortere, *A Different God*, 33.

10. See ibid., 34.

11. Ibid., 33.

12. Ibid., 34.

13. Ibid., 36.

14. Ibid., 37.

15. Ibid., 37–38.

16. For example, see Sara K. Pinnock, *Beyond Theodicy: Jewish and Christian Continental Thinkers Respond to the Holocaust* (Albany: State University of New York Press, 2002), 113–27.

17. Depoortere, *A Different God*, 39–42.

18. See ibid., 41.

19. Ibid.

20. Ibid., 43.

21. Ibid., 45.

22. Ibid., 42.

23. Ibid., 47.

24. Ibid., 45.

25. Soelle takes this logic to an extreme, contending that once we establish God as omnipotent, the very God to whom the sufferer wishes to turn for comfort is the One inflicting the suffering (Soelle, *Suffering*, 17–28).

5. Apathy as a Response to Suffering

1. Jaime Bailleres, photographer, in Charles Bowden, Noam Chomsky, and Eduardo Galeano, *Juárez: The Laboratory of Our Future* (New York: Aperture, 1998).

2. The Latin word *acedia* derives from the Greek *akedes* meaning "indifferent" or "careless." See Aviad Kleinberg, *Seven Deadly Sins: A Very Partial List* (Cambridge, MA: Harvard University Press, 2008), 32.

3. Evagrius Ponticus, *The Praktikos Chapters on Prayer* (Kalamazoo, MI: Cistercian Publications, 1981), 18.

4. See Kathleen Norris, *A Marriage, Monks, and a Writer's Life: Acedia and Me* (New York: Riverhead Books, 2008), 5.

5. Kleinberg, *Seven Deadly Sins*, 32–43.

6. Rollo May, *Love and Will* (New York: W. W. Norton and Company, 1969), 29.

7. Ibid., 28, 31.

8. Ibid., 33.

9. Ibid., 28.

10. Dorothee Soelle, *Suffering* (Philadelphia: Fortress Press, 1973), 36–37.

11. Ibid., 36–38.

12. Ibid., 37, 39.

13. Ikmulisa Livingston, John Doyle, and Dan Mangan, "Stabbed Hero Dies as More than 20 People Stroll Past Him," *New York Post* (April 25, 2010).

14. Bibb Latané and John M. Darley, *The Unresponsive Bystander: Why Doesn't He Help* (New York: Appleton-Century-Crofts, 1970), 4.

15. Ibid., 38, 40.

16. Soelle, *Suffering*, 39.

17. May, *Love and Will*, 31.

18. Soelle, *Suffering*, 38.

19. Ibid., 40.

20. May, *Love and Will*, 31.

21. Ponticus, *The Praktikos Chapters on Prayer*, 26.

22. May, *Love and Will,* 110–11.

23. Soelle, *Suffering*, 40.

24. May, *Love and Will*, 30.

25. Cf. ibid., 28.

26. Ibid., 30–31.

6. Is There a Suffering God?

1. According to Harold S. Kushner, "Christianity introduces the world to the idea of a God who suffers, alongside the image of a God who creates and commands. Post-biblical Judaism also occasionally spoke of a God who suffers, a God who is made homeless and goes into exile along with His people, a God who weeps when He sees what some of His children are doing to other of His children. I don't believe that God is a person like me, with real eyes and real tear ducts to cry, and real nerve endings to feel pain. But I would like to think that the anguish I feel when I read of the suffering of innocent people reflects God's anguish and God's compassion, even if His way of feeling pain is different from ours. I would like to think that He is the source of

my being able to feel sympathy and outrage, and that He and I are on the same side when we stand with the victim against those who would hurt him" (*When Bad Things Happen to Good People* [New York: Anchor Books, 2004], 95).

2. Elie Wiesel, *Night* (New York: Avon Books, 1969), 74–75.

3. Cf. Sarah K. Pinnock, *Beyond Theodicy: Jewish and Christian Continental Thinkers Respond to the Holocaust* (Albany: State University of New York Press, 2002), 89.

4. Soelle offers an interpretation of this scene based on the Jewish understanding of the Hebrew term *shekhinah*. In Hebrew, *shekhinah* has complex meanings and interpretations, but most often refers to the "indwelling" presence of God. Jews also understand it to mean "the glory of God," often realized in the dramatic theophanies of biblical times. Near the end of the Book of Exodus, for example, Yahweh takes possession of the sanctuary in a mysterious cloud. The biblical text describes *shekhinah*: "the glory of Yahweh filled the tabernacle" (Ex 40:35). This overwhelming manifestation prevents Moses from entering the holy place. For modern-day Jews, *shekhinah* holds a more familiar place. For example, it is the divine presence in Sabbath gatherings (see Dorothee Soelle, *Suffering* [Philadelphia: Fortress Press, 1975], 145–50).

5. Pinnock, *Beyond Theodicy*, 89.

6. Ibid., 83.

7. Richard Bauckham, "'Only the Suffering God Can Help': Divine Possibility in Modern Theology," *Themelios* 9, no. 3 (April 1984): 6–12, also theologicalstudies.org.uk website.

8. Ibid.

9. Ibid. As Bauckham notes, "If the Fathers are to be criticized, it is not, of course, for the necessary attempt to make some connection between the biblical God and the God of Greek philosophy, but for the insufficiently critical nature of their reconciliation between the two. They retain the most important features of the biblical God, but do not allow these features sufficient scope in calling into question the philosophical notion of divine nature."

10. Bauckham explains that "tensions in the patristic doctrine of God arose especially in the attempt to reconcile the immutability and impassibility of God with the Fathers' belief in a real incarnation of

God in Christ and in the real suffering of Christ, to both of which they held tenaciously as Christian theologians, in spite of the problems created by their Greek philosophical presupposition about the divine nature" (ibid.). See also J. K. Mozley, *The Impassibility of God* (Cambridge: Cambridge University Press, 1926).

11. Bauckham, "'Only the Suffering God Can Help.'"

12. Deism rose as the star of the Age of Enlightenment, primarily in France and England. In the United States many of the Founding Fathers were deists, such as Benjamin Franklin, Thomas Jefferson, George Washington, and Thomas Paine. Since the eighteenth century the dominant understanding of divinity has been deistic, with many popular strains of deism flourishing today.

13. The assumption of the deist view of divinity and the world is that a higher intelligence must have created complexity because matter is inert. Therefore, the act of creation is the direct act of the Divine.

14. See Bauckham, "'Only the Suffering God Can Help.'"

15. A. J. Heschel, *The Prophets* (New York: Jewish Publication Society of America, 1962), 241, 257.

16. Fear of the patripassian heresy confined traditional theological reflection on the suffering of the cross to Jesus. Patripassianism argued that God the Father suffers because he was incarnate—and so whatever the Son experienced, so too did the Father. For example, Praxeas, who lived at the end of the second and beginning of the third centuries, taught that "the Father Himself descended into the Virgin, Himself was born of her, Himself died, in short that He Himself was Jesus Christ" (in Mozley, *The Impassibility of God*, 30). Thus the patripassian stance that the Father became a co-sufferer at the crucifixion heretically opposes the Hellenistic theological understanding of divine apathy. Moltmann, in search of a humane and relevant theology of a suffering God, recasts traditional theological understandings of the relations among the persons of the Trinity in light of the crucifixion in a manner that avoids the heretical patripassian pitfalls (Jürgen Moltmann, *The Crucified God: The Cross of Christ as the Foundation and Criticism of Christian Theology* [Minneapolis, MN: Fortress Press, 1993]; see also Mozley, *The Impassibility of God*, 29–36.)

17. Moltmann, *The Crucified God*, 204. See also Bauckham, "Only the Suffering God Can Help."

18. In concepts of earlier systematic theology, it is possible to talk of a *homoousion* with respect to God, and thus of the community of will of the Father and the Son on the cross. However, the unity contains not only identity of substance but also the wholly and utterly different character and inequality of the event on the cross. In the cross, Father and Son are most deeply separated in forsakenness and, at the same time, are most inwardly one in their surrender (cf. Moltmann, *The Crucified God*, 244).

19. Moltmann, *The Crucified God*, 243.

20. Ibid., 242.

21. As Moltmann explains, "For Jesus suffers dying in forsakenness, but not death itself; for men can no longer 'suffer' death, because suffering presupposes life. But the Father who abandons him and delivers him up suffers the death of the Son in the infinite grief of love. We cannot therefore say there in patripassian terms that the Father suffered and died. The suffering and dying of the Son, forsaken by the Father, is a different kind of suffering from the suffering of the Father in the death of the Son" (ibid., 244).

22. Ibid., 244, 206–7.

23. The foundation of this theological concept is an ancient Israelite understanding of those who were "delivered up." This phrase was employed, for example, in Jesus' passion narrative and carries with it the negative connotation of "hand over, give up, deliver, betray, cast out, kill" (ibid., 241). The Israelites understood God as delivering sinners up to corruption of their own choosing and abandoning them in their forsakenness. This ancient understanding of being "delivered up" connotes two conjoined levels of abandonment: those "who abandon God are [in turn] abandoned by God."

24. Moltmann's theology is grounded in Paul's emphatic statement that the Father "delivers up" his Son on the cross. Although Paul distantly echoes the ancient Israelite understanding, he is introducing a radical shift in what it means to be "delivered up." The deliverance of Jesus to death signifies that he became sin for the salvation of others. Pauline theology understands deliverance as involving several interrelated aspects. In Romans, Paul asks, "Is it possible that he who did not spare his own Son but handed him over for the sake of us all will not grant us all things besides?" (Rom 8:31). Paul argues here for the

overwhelming love of God for sinners, that no cost was too weighty for their salvation, even the life of the Son. Thus it is the Father who enacted deliverance of the Son. Pauline logic contends that if the Father was willing to make such a sacrifice for sinners, there can be no doubt of the Father's forgiveness of them. For this deliverance of sinners to occur, the Son became "accursed." Paul writes, "For us, as it is written: 'Accursed is anyone who is hanged on a tree'" (Gal 3:13). In 2 Corinthians he clarifies the point: "For our sakes God made him who did not know sin, to be sin, so that in him we might become the very holiness of God" (2 Cor 5:21). Jesus took on the sin of humanity through his deliverance, and in so doing, gained our salvation.

25. Moltmann, *The Crucified God*, 242.

26. Ibid., 252, 242.

27. Moltmann, *The Crucified God*, 252.

28. Alfred North Whitehead, *Process and Reality: An Essay in Cosmology* (New York: Harper and Brothers, 1957), 532.

29. Moltmann, *The Crucified God*, 46, as quoted in Bauckham, "'Only the Suffering God Can Help.'"

30. Moltmann, *The Crucified God*, 46.

31. Ibid., 53.

32. Moltmann, *Experience of God*, trans. Margaret Kohl (Minneapolis, MN: Fortress Press, 2007), 53.

33. Robert Ellsberg, "Dorothee Soelle," in *All Saints: Daily Reflections on Saints, Prophets, and Witnesses for Our Time* (New York: Crossroad, 1997).

34. Soelle writes, "My first engagement of suffering as a place of mystical experience took place some twenty-five years ago when I wrote the book *Suffering*. . . . I distanced myself from all Christian masochism as well as apathy, which as the inability to suffer resides in the belief in process" (*The Silent Cry: Mysticism and Resistance*, trans. Barbara and Martin Rumscheidt [Minneapolis, MN: Fortress Press, 2001], 133).

35. Ibid., 133–55.

36. Ibid., 26–27.

37. Ibid., 26.

38. "Masochism's presuppositions that God is almighty (proposition one), and loving and just (proposition two), lead to the conclusion that

all suffering serves with to punish, test, or train" (Soelle, *Suffering,* 24). It is characterized by "the low value it places on human strength; its veneration of one who is neither good nor logical but only extremely powerful; its viewing of suffering exclusively from the perspective of endurance; and its consequent lack of sensitivity for the suffering of others" (ibid., 22).

39. Ibid., 21.

40. I develop two of Soelle's appropriate responses to suffering, lament, and acceptance in the next chapter.

41. Soelle critiques the theological companion piece of a masochistic spirituality, which is the sadist God. She summarizes the logic of this spirituality in three points: "(1) God is the almighty ruler of the world and he sends all suffering; (2) God acts justly not capriciously; and (3) all suffering is punishment for sin." For Soelle, this is a "God who produces suffering and causes affliction." She laments that this spirituality has become a "glorious theme" of theology that "directs our attention to the God who demands the impossible and tortures people." This spirituality prioritizes the abysmal depravity of humanity, with the implication of a God who receives some pleasure from human chastisement. Soelle cautions that "any attempt to look upon suffering as caused directly or indirectly by God stands in danger of regarding him as sadistic" (ibid., 22–26).

42. Soelle observes that theologies of sadism school Christians in disturbing patterns of behavior that are understood as normative. These forms of Christianity, she says, "school people in thought patterns that regard sadistic behavior as normal, in which one worships, honors, and loves a being whose 'radicality,' 'intentionality,' and 'greatest sharpness' is that he slays" (ibid., 28).

43. Ibid., 146, 148.

44. Ibid.

45. Johann Baptist Metz, "Communicating a Dangerous Memory," in *Communicating a Dangerous Memory: Soundings in Political Theology,* ed. Fred Lawrence (Atlanta: Scholars Press, 1987), 39–40.

46. Ekkehard Schuster and Reinhold Boschert-Kimmig, *Hope against Hope: Johann Baptist Metz and Elie Wiesel Speak Out on the Holocaust*, trans. J. Matthew Ashley (New York: A Stimulus Book, 1999), 4.

47. Ashley, *Interruptions,* 27–28.

48. Ibid., 29.

49. Ibid., 27–28.

50. See Rebecca S. Chopp, "Johann Baptist Metz: The Subject of Suffering," *The Praxis of Suffering: An Interpretation of Liberation and Political Theologies* (Eugene, OR: Wipf and Stock, 1986), 64–65.

51. Johann Baptist Metz, *A Passion for God: The Mystical-Political Dimension of Christianity*, trans. J. Matthew Ashley (New York: Paulist Press, 1990), 56.

52. Ashley, *Interruptions*, 27–28.

53. The entire quotation merits our attention: "The discussion revolves around the suffering God, the suffering between God and God. I myself cannot follow this tendency. And let me here name my most important reservation: Is no reconciliation with God at work here that is too speculative, too proximate to Gnosis, achieved too much behind the back of the human history of suffering? Is there not also especially for theologians that negative mystery of human suffering which will not allow itself to be made sense of in anyone's name? How is discourse on the suffering God not just a sublime duplication of human suffering and human powerlessness?" (Johann Baptist Metz and J. Matthew Ashley, "Suffering unto God," *Critical Inquiry* 20, no. 4, Symposium on "God" [Summer 1994]: 619).

54. Ashley, *Interruptions*, 29.

55. Johann Baptist Metz, *Faith in History and Society: Toward a Practical Fundamental Theology*, trans. and ed. J. Matthew Ashley (New York: Herder and Herder, 2007), 87–96; see also Metz, "Communicating a Dangerous Memory," 37–53.

56. Metz, *A Passion for God*, 56.

57. Johannes Baptist Metz, *Poverty of Spirit*, trans. John Drury (New York: Newman Press, 1998), 10.

58. Metz, *Faith in History and Society*, 89.

59. Ibid., 227.

60. Metz and Ashley, "Suffering unto God," 619.

61. Metz, *Poverty of Spirit*, 38.

62. See Pinnock, *Beyond Theodicy*, 94–95.

63. Metz, *Faith in History and Society*, 84.

64. Pinnock, *Beyond Theodicy*, 83. See also Schuster and Boschert-Kimmig, *Hope against Hope*.

65. Soelle, *Suffering*, 91.

66. For other examples of *go'el*, see 2 Samuel 14:11 and Isaiah 43:14; 41:14; 44:24; 52:3–9. With regard to the interpretation and translation of the Book of Job, Kushner comment on this key verse: "The familiar statement of faith 'I know that my Redeemer lives,' may mean instead 'I would rather be redeemed while I am still alive" (*When Bad Things Happen to Good People*, 37). Gutiérrez acknowledges that this "much-studied passage . . . makes for the reading difficult and therefore susceptible of substantially different translations."Yet Gutiérrez says, "In my view, he [Job] is referring to God. . . . Job's cry expresses an anguished but sure hope" (Gustavo Gutiérrez, *On Job: God-Talk and the Suffering of the Innocent* [Maryknoll, NY: Orbis Books, 1987], 64–65).

67. Gutiérrez, *On Job*, 64–65.

68. Ibid., 64, 65.

69. Ibid., 65–66.

70. On this point Gutiérrez quotes Robert Gordis: "Actually, the problem arises only because of the tendency to apply Western logic to the Oriental spirit. The sharp delimitation of personality is foreign to biblical thought. In all these passages, Job is affirming his faith that behind the God of violence, so tragically manifested in the world, stand the God of righteousness and love—and they are not two but one! Thus Job's attack upon conventional religion is actually the expression of deepest trust. Hence Job is eminently worthy of God's final encomium pronounced upon him" (ibid., 121n17).

71. Pinnock, *Beyond Theodicy*. See also Schuster and Boschert-Kimmig, *Hope against Hope*, 113. Pinnock bases her critique on the work of two feminists theologians: Flora Keshgegian, *Redeeming Memories: A Theology of Healing and Transformation* (Nashville, TN: Abingdon Press, 2000), 121–25; and Sharon D. Welch, *Communities of Resistance and Solidarity: A Feminist Theology of Liberation* (Maryknoll, NY: Orbis Books, 1985), 35–42.

7. Responses to Suffering

1. "Esther Chávez,"Telegraph.co.uk (January 26, 2010).

2. Alfredo Corchano, "Esther Chávez Cano: Became Leading Voice on Killings in Juárez, Mexico," *Dallas News* (December 29, 2009).

3. "Ciudad Juarez Women's Rights Activist Esther Chávez Dies," *Latin American Herald Tribune* (n.d.).

4. Bobby Byrd, "Esther Chávez Cano (1933–2009)," blog.

5. Kent Paterson, "Femicide Fighter, Esther Chávez Cano, Honored by New Mexico State University," *La Prensa San Diego* (November 21, 2007).

6. Ibid.

7. Ibid.

8. Byrd, "Esther Chávez Cano (1933–2009)."

9. Paterson, "Femicide Fighter, Esther Chávez Cano, Honored by New Mexico State University."

10. Ibid.

11. Ibid.

12. Byrd, "Esther Chávez Cano (1933–2009)."

13. "Ciudad Juarez Women's Rights Activist Esther Chávez Dies."

14. Corchano, "Esther Chávez Cano."

15. Tracy Wilkinson, "Esther Chávez Dies at 76: Activist Decried Murder of Women in Ciudad Juárez," *Los Angeles Times* (December 27, 2009).

16. Corchano, "Esther Chávez Cano."

17. Byrd, "Esther Chávez Cano (1933–2009)."

18. Jose Luis Magana, photograph (© 2003), reprinted in Wilkinson, "Esther Chávez Dies at 76."

19. Corchano, "Esther Chávez Cano."

20. Wilkinson, "Esther Chávez Dies at 76."

21. Dorothee Soelle, *Suffering* (Philadelphia: Fortress Press, 1975), 69.

22. The Catholic baptismal rite recalls both the coming reign of God and Mark's *ephaphatha* miracle story, integrating its tactual expression and even the *ephaphatha* command. The priest touches the ears and lips of the newly baptized and prays: "The Lord made the deaf to hear and the dumb to speak. May he soon touch your ears to receive his word, and your mouth to proclaim his faith, to the praise and glory of God the Father" (*The Rites of the Catholic Church* [New York: Pueblo Publishing Co., 1976], 210).

23. Soelle, *Suffering*, 68–70.

24. John S. Kselman, SS, and Michael L. Barré, "Psalms," *The New Jerome Biblical Commentary*, ed. Raymond E. Brown, SS, Joseph A.

Fitzmyer, SJ, and Roland E. Murphy, OCarm (Englewood Cliffs, NJ: Prentice Hall, 1990), 525.

25. Ibid.

26. See "Madres de jóvenes desaparecidas, *Regeneración* (May 11, 2011). This magazine's Spanish-language website—regeneracion. mx—offers other key links to the feminicides and other human rights issues.

27. My translation.

28. Richard Bauckham, "'Only the Suffering God Can Help': Divine Possibility in Modern Theology," *Themelios* 9, no. 3 (April 1984): 6–12; see also theologicalstudies.org.uk website.

29. Soelle, *Suffering*, 91–92.

30. Ibid., 91.

31. Ibid.

32. *Mysterium* refers to the experience of a reality that is perceived as beyond our capacity fully to understand. It is "outstanding" or extraordinary, and thus "that which is ever greater." *Tremendum* denotes an uncanny feeling of peculiar dread before the "ever greater mystery." *Fascinans* signifies the awe that accompanies the experience of mystery (see Rudolf Otto, *The Idea of the Holy*, trans. John W. Harvey [London: Oxford University Press, 1950]).

Epilogue

1. John of the Cross, *The Ascent of Mount Carmel*, in *The Collected Works of St. John of the Cross*, trans. Kieran Kavanaugh, OCD, and Otilio Rodriguez, OCD (Washington, DC: ICS Publications, 1979), bk. 1, chap. 2, vol. 1.

Bibliography

Theological Philosophical Works

The Anchor Bible: Mark. Translated by C. S. Mann. New York: Doubleday, 1986.

Baum, Gregory, ed. *The Twentieth Century: A Theological Overview*. Maryknoll, NY: Orbis Books, 1999.

Brown, Raymond E., Joseph A. Fitzmyer, and Roland E. Murphy, eds. *The New Jerome Biblical Commentary*. Englewood Cliffs, NJ: Prentice Hall, 1990.

Bynum, Caroline Walker. *Fragmentation and Redemption: Essays on Gender and the Human Body in Medieval Religion*. New York: Zone Books, 1992.

————. *Holy Feast and Holy Fast: The Religious Significance of Food to Medieval Women*. Berkeley and Los Angeles: University of California Press, 1987.

Crossan, John Dominic. *The Dark Interval: Toward a Theology of Story*. Sonoma, CA: Polebridge Press, 1988.

Delumeau, Jean. *Sin and Fear: The Emergence of a Western Guilt Culture, 13th–18th Centuries*. Translated by Eric Nicholson. New York: St. Martin's Press, 1990.

De Unamuno, Miguel. *Tragic Sense of Life*. Translated by J. E. Crawford Flitch. New York: Dover Publications, 2010.

Duquoc, Christian. "Demonism and the Unexpectedness of God." *Concilium* 184 (1983).

Ellison, John W. *Nelson's Complete Concordance and the Revised Standard Version Bible*. New York: Thomas Nelson and Sons, 1957.

Flannery, Austin, ed. *Vatican Council II: The Conciliar and Post Conciliar Documents*. Northport, NY: Costello Publishing Company, 1998.

Goldberg, Michael. *Theology and Narrative: A Critical Introduction*. Eugene, OR: Wipf and Stock Publishers, 2001.

Gutiérrez, Gustavo. *On Job, God-Talk, and the Suffering of the Innocent.* Translated by Matthew J. O'Connell. Maryknoll, NY: Orbis Books, 1985.

————. *A Theology of Liberation: History, Politics, and Salvation.* Translated by Caridad Inda and John Eagleson. Maryknoll, NY: Orbis Books, 1994.

Hall, Douglas John. *God and Human Suffering: An Exercise in the Theology of the Cross.* Minneapolis, MN: Augsburg Publishing House, 1986.

Hauerwas, Stanley, and L. Gregory Jones, ed. *Why Narrative?: Readings in Narrative Theology.* Eugene, OR: Wipf and Stock Publishers, 1997.

Heschel, Abraham J. *The Prophets.* New York: Harper and Row, 1962.

Kitamori, Kiazoh. *The Theology of the Pain of God.* Translated by Kami No Itami No Shingaku. Eugene, OR: Wipf and Stock Publishers, 1958.

Kushner, Harold S. *When Bad Things Happen to Good People.* New York: Quill, 2001.

Lewis, C. S. *The Problem of Pain / A Grief Observed.* Nashville, TN: Broadman and Holman, 1999.

Metz, Johann Baptist. "Facing the Jews: Christian Theology after Auschwitz." *Concilium* 175 (1984): 26–33.

————. *Faith in History and Society: Toward a Fundamental Theology.* Translated by J. Matthew Ashley. New York: Herder and Herder, 2007.

————. "The Future in the Memory of Suffering." *Concilium* 76 (1972): 9–25.

Moltmann, Jürgen. *The Crucified God: The Cross of Christ as the Foundation and Criticism of Christian Theology.* Minneapolis, MN: Fortress Press, 1993.

————. *Experiences of God.* Minneapolis, MN: Fortress Press, 2007.

————. *The Theology of Hope: On the Ground and the Implications of a Christian Eschatology.* Minneapolis, MN: Fortress Press, 1993.

————. *The Trinity and the Kingdom: The Doctrine of God.* Minneapolis, MN: Fortress Press, 1993.

Mozley, J. K. *The Impassibility of God: A Survey of Christian Thought.* Cambridge: The University Press, 1926.

Norris, Kathleen. *A Marriage, Monks, and a Writer's Life: Acedia and Me.* New York: Riverhead Books, 2008.

Pinnock, Sarah K. *Beyond Theodicy: Jewish and Christian Continental Thinkers Respond to the Holocaust*. Albany: State University of New York Press, 2002.

Poticus, Evagrius. *The Praktikos and Chapters on Prayer*. Translated by John Eudes Bamberger. Kalamazoo, MI: Cistercian Publications, 1981.

Rahner, Karl. *Encounters with Silence*. Translated by James M. Demske. South Bend, IN: St. Augustine's Press, 1999.

———. *Foundations of Christian Faith: An Introduction to the Idea of Christianity*. Translated by William V. Dych. New York: Crossroad, 1993.

Ricoeur, Paul. *The Symbolism of Evil*. Translated by Emerson Buchanan. Boston: Beacon Press, 1967.

Schüssler Fiorenza, Elisabeth. *Wisdom Ways: Introducing Feminist Biblical Interpretations*. Maryknoll, NY: Orbis Books, 2005.

Soelle, Dorothee. *Revolutionary Patience*. Translated by Rita Kimber and Robert Kimber. Eugene, OR: Wipf and Stock Publishers, 1974.

———. *The Silent Cry: Mysticism and Resistance*, Minneapolis, MN: Fortress Press, 2001.

———. *Suffering*. Translated by Everett R. Kalin. Philadelphia: Fortress Press, 1975.

———. *Theology of Skeptics: Reflections on God*. Translated by Joyce L. Irwin. Minneapolis, MN: Fortress Press, 1995.

Tracy, David. *The Analogical Imagination: Christian Theology and the Culture of Pluralism*. New York: Crossroad, 1991.

———. *On Naming the Present: God, Hermeneutics, and Church*. Maryknoll, NY: Orbis Books, 1994.

Weil, Simone. *Waiting for God*. Translated by Emma Craufurd. New York: Harper Perennial Modern Classics, 2009.

Wiesel, Elie. *Wise Men and Their Tales: Portraits of Biblical, Talmudic, and Hasidic Masters*. New York: Schocken Books, 2003.

Interdisciplinary Works

Acosta, Mariclaire. "The Women of Ciudad Juárez." University of California, Berkeley: Center for Latin American Studies, 2005. Electronic document, http://www.escholarship.org/uc/item/1625t8mr.

Albuquerque, Pedro H., and Prasad R. Vemala. "A Statistical Evaluation of Femicide Rates in Mexican Cities along the US-Mexico

Border" (October 5, 2008). Canadian Law and Economics Association (CLEA) 2008 Meetings, 2008. Available at SSRN, http://ssrn.com/abstract=1112308.

Anzaldúa, Gloria. *Borderlands*, La Frontera. *The New Mestiza*. San Francisco: Aunt Lute Books, 1987.

Bosworth, Barry, and Susan M. Collin. *Coming Together, Mexico-United State Relations*. Washington, DC: Brookings Institution Press, 1997.

Bowden, Charles. *Down by the River*. New York: Simon and Schuster, 2004.

———. *Juárez: The Laboratory of Our Future*. New York: Aperture Foundation, 1998.

———. *Murder City: Cuidad Juárez and the Global Economy's New Killing Fields*. New York: Nation Books, 2010.

Byrd, Bobby, and Susannah Mississippi Byrd, eds. *The Later Great Mexican Border*. El Paso, TX: Cinco Punto Press, 1996.

Campbell, Howard. *Drug War Zone: Frontline Dispatches from the Streets of El Paso and Juárez*. Austin: University of Texas Press, 2009.

———. "Female Drug Smugglers on the U.S.-Mexico Border: Gender, Crime and Empowerment," *Anthropological Quarterly* 81, no. 1 (2008): 233–67.

Carpenter, Ted Galen. "Mexico Is Becoming the Next Colombia." Foreign Policy Briefing, Cato Institute, no. 87, November 15, 2005.

Di Palma, Giuseppe. *Apathy and Participation: Mass Politics in Western Societies*. New York: The Free Press, 1970.

Frankel, Viktor E. *Man's Search for Meaning*. New York: Pocket Books, 1985.

Fregoso, Linda Rosa. "Femicide: The Case of Ciudad Juarez, Mexico, 1993–1999." Electronic document, http://www.nursinglibrary.org/Portal/main.aspx?pageid=4024andsid=20290.

———. *Mexicana Encounters*. Berkeley and Los Angeles: University of California Press, 2003.

———. "Voices without Echo: The Global Gendered Apartheid."

———. *Emergences: Journal for the Study of Media and Composite Cultures* 10, no. 1 (2000): 137–55.

Freud, Sigmund. *Civilization and Its Discontents*. Translated by James Strachey. New York: W. W. Norton and Company, 1961.

Gaspar de Alba, Alicia. "The Maquiladora Murders, 1993–2003." *Aztlán: A Journal of Chicano Studies* 28 no. 3 (Fall 2003): 1–17.

Gutman, Matthew C. *The Meanings of Macho: Being a Man in Mexico City*. Berkeley and Los Angeles: University of California Press, 2007.

Kristof, Nicholas D., and Sheryl WuDunn. *Half the Sky: Turning Oppression into Opportunity for Women Worldwide*. New York: Alfred A. Knopf, 2009.

Latané, Bibb, and John M. Darley. *The Unresponsive Bystander: Why Doesn't He Help?* New York: Appleton-Chuturey-Crofts, 1970.

May, Rollo. *Love and Will*. New York: W. W. Norton and Company, 1969.

———. *Man's Search for Himself*. New York: W. W. Norton and Company, 1953.

Narayan, Uma. *Dislocating Cultures: Identities, Traditions, and Third-World Feminism*. New York: Routledge, 1997.

Nathan, Debbie. "Death Comes to the Maquilas: A Border Story." *The Nation* 264, no. 2 (January 13–20, 2003): 18–22.

Payan, Tony. "The Drug War and the U.S.-Mexico Border: The State of Affairs." *South Atlantic Quarterly* 105, no. 4 (Fall 2006): 863–80.

Paz, Octavio. *The Labyrinth of Solitude and Other Writings*. New York: Grove Press, 1985.

Radford, Jill, and Diana E. H. Russell, eds. *Femicide: The Politics of Women Killing*. New York: Twayne Publishers, 1992.

Russell, Diana E. H., and Roberta A. Harmes, eds. *Femicide in Global Perspective*. New York: Teachers College Press, 2001.

Schüssler Fiorenza, Elisabeth. *Wisdom Ways: Introducing Feminist Biblical Interpretation*. Maryknoll, NY: Orbis Books, 2005.

Segura, Denise A., and Patricia Zavella, eds. *Women and Migration in the U.S.-Mexico Borderlands: A Reader*. Durham, NC: Duke University Press, 2007.

Solomon, Marion F., and Daniel J. Siegel, eds. *Healing Trauma: Attachment, Mind, Body, and Brain*. New York: W. W. Norton and Company, 2003.

Staudt, Kathleen, César M. Fuentes, and Julia E. Monárrez Fragoso, eds. *Cities and Citizenship at the U.S.-Mexico Border: The Paso del Norte Metropolitan Region*. New York: Palgrave Macmillan, 2010.

———. *Violence and Activism at the Border: Gender, Fear, and Everyday Life in Ciudad Juárez*. Austin: University of Texas Press. 2008.

Stevens, Evelyn P. "*Marianismo*: The Other Face of *Machismo* in Latin America." In *Female and Male in Latin America*, edited by Ann Pescatello, 82–102. Pittsburgh: University of Pittsburgh Press, 1973.

Tillich, Paul. *The Courage to Be*. New Haven, CT: Yale University Press, 2000.

Townes, Emilie M. *Womanist Ethics and the Cultural Production of Evil*. New York: Palgrave Macmillan, 2006.

Urrea, Luis Alberto, *The Devil's Highway: A True Story*. New York: Back Bay Books, 2004.

Valdez, Diana Washington. *The Killing Fields, Harvest of Women*. Burbank, CA: Peace at the Border, 2006.

Volk, Steven S., and Marian E. Schlotterbeck. "Gender, Order, and Femicide, Reading the Popular Culture of Murder in Ciudad Juárez." *Aztlán: A Journal of Chicago Studies* 32, no. 1 (Spring 2007): 53–86.

Wilson, Patricia A. *Exports and Local Development, Mexico's New Maquiladoras*. Austin: University of Texas Press, 1992.

Wright, Melissa W. "The Dialectics of Still Life: Murder, Women and Maquiladoras." In *Women and Migration in the U.S.–Mexico Borderlands*, edited by Denise A. Segura and Patricia Zavella. Durham, NC: Duke University Press, 2007.

————. *Disposable Women and Other Myths of Global Capitalism: Perspectives on Gender*. New York: Taylor and Francis Group, 2006.

————. "Feminine Villains, Masculine Heroes, and the Reproduction of Ciudad Juárez." *Social Text* 19, no. 4 (Winter 2001): 93–113.

Fiction and Memoir

Bolano, Roberto. *2666*. Translated by Natasha Wimmer. New York: Farrar, Straus, and Giroux, 2004.

Garcia Marquez, Gabriel. *News of a Kidnapping*. Translated by Edith Grossman. New York: Alfred A. Knopf, 1997.

Gaspar de Alba, Alicia. *Desert Blood: The Juárez Murders*. Houston, TX: Arte Público Press, 2005.

Lusseyran, Jacques. *And There Was Light: The Autobiography of a Blind Hero in the French Resistance*. Translated by Elizabeth R. Cameron. Boston: Floris Books, 2007.

Rodriguez, Teresa, with Diana Montané. *The Daughters of Juárez*. New York: Atria Books, 2007.